Advance Praise for
Even If Your Toes Turn Purple

*"This book has changed the way I am raising my children and gives
me hope and excitement for our Millennials. It teaches parents how to
foster entrepreneurship, achievement, gratitude, and generosity—all in a
captivating narrative that will entertain as well as educate."*

—GARRETT GUNDERSON
New York Times Bestselling Author of *Killing Sacred Cows*,
Founder of Inc 500 firm

*"The values taught in these short and engaging stories were captivating
and informative. The perspectives offered from both the teen and his parents
were powerful and insightful. For any anxious mother and father, this
extraordinary book will provide the reader with thoughtful guidelines for
rearing confident, happy, and successful children."*

—ALAN HALL
Chairman of MarketStar Corporation

*"The Christiansens are an example of how supporting each other, teaching
traditional values, and engaging in fun, adventurous activities together
strengthens a family and encourages individual uniqueness. This book is full
of sound principles for all families."*

—RICK MAW
Co-founder of ValuesParenting.com

"This book not only gave me hope in the 'fearless abilities' of Millennials, but also made me realize there is still a teenager inside of me. I always say 'I'm not my age, I'm my heartbeat.'"

—CATHY L. GREENBERG, PH.D.
Wall Street Journal and *New York Times* Bestselling Author of
Fearless Leaders: Sharpen Your Focus

"If you're passionate about raising strong, independent, and purpose-driven kids who win big in business and life then this book is a MUST! Our children will absolutely go in the direction we guide them, and this book provides a powerful insight into how to do exactly that!"

—KAT LOTERZO
Author, speaker, and success coach

"As Even If Your Toes Turn Purple *teaches, whether climbing mountains, building businesses, or serving others with empathy, all three share the same core values. A clear vision, confidence in yourself and others, and most importantly the ability to communicate openly with your team. This book will teach you how to strengthen trust with your children, and I am wiser today for having read it. Thank you, Rich.*"

—JOHN WALBRECHT
President of Black Diamond Equipment, father of two

"This book and message should be read by parents raising entrepreneurial kids."

—GREG REID
Founder of Secret Knock business conference,
bestselling author of *Think and Grow Rich* series

"Rich hits the head on the nail when he talks about the sticky subjects that we should be talking to our kids about. His book helped me with a paradigm shift of how to talk to our kids and why we should. This book is a very hopeful and fresh perspective on raising our kids to be responsible and hard working. I loved the insight into how to teach our kids to be entrepreneurs and helping them to understand money and how to manage it. This book is a must read if you feel that the teenage years have to be hard."

—DESI WARD
Founder of The Mom Conference and Unconventional Kitchen

"Good parenting is one of the most difficult, yet vitally important responsibilities. Kudos to Rich and Tim for giving us such a fantastic and heartfelt resource. Rich attacks this book with the same enthusiasm and energy he is famous for and hits another home run!"

—BRETT D. CHRISTIANSEN, M.D.

"In today's tech-driven society, Even If Your Toes Turn Purple narrows the parent-teen gap by teaching timeless principles through real-life and artful storytelling. It's a must read for any parent looking to make a lifelong connection with their teen."

—CURTIS BLAIR
CEO of Froghair, Co-founder at Hoodoo Capital

"We all want to help our kids to be successful, productive, and happy, and Rich has found the right way to do it. His approach isn't pushy, and it isn't demanding—it's simply effective."

—LYNN ABPLANALP
Sr. VP of Temkin International, youth advocate and leader

"Rich's new book is a great template for how to raise successful teens in this day and age. Each chapter had straightforward principles and easy-to-implement action steps for parents and kids. As a business and relationship coach, it's distressing to see so many parents today still struggling with how to teach their kids about money, intimacy, and how to succeed in life. I am so grateful that Rich and Tim have put together a practical study guide for today's families that can initiate effective discussions and real results. I truly believe that following these principals will create a powerful and honest relationship with your teenager, while bringing out the best in them as well. I highly recommend this book to all parents looking to master the art of parenting."

—DINO WATTS, PH.D.
Bestselling author of The Practice RX

"Even If Your Toes Turn Purple is an incredible vehicle for looking at parenting with new hope and excitement. Rich and Tim (with Alex and Alice) have masterfully weaved storytelling with concepts that parents and teenagers alike can immediately use. The breakthrough theories revealed in this book are easily understood and the takeaways are profound. While absorbing the concepts in this book, not only did I have multiple 'ah-hah' moments, but I also found myself saying, 'So THIS is how the Christiansens have managed to help mold their teenagers into such incredible adults.' This book will enlighten you and reinforce your understanding of the 'MUST DOS' in raising teenagers who are confident, happy, and stand out."

—NANCY SINGLETON
Co-founder of Singleton Systems

"This book is hands down the best parenting book I have ever read. Rich shares his perspective and advice through captivating stories that educate as well as entertain. Not only did I learn from these stories myself, but I can also share them with my children to teach them in a way that they will listen."

—AMY OSMOND COOK, PH.D.
CEO of Osmond Marketing

Even if your
toes turn
purple

Even if your toes turn purple

Raising Teenagers That Are
Confident, Happy, and **Stand Out**

Rich & Tim Christiansen

Except as permitted under the U.S. Copyright Act of 1976, no part of this publication may be used or reproduced without the prior written permission of the publisher, Sourced Media Books, LLC, 15 Via Picato, San Clemente, CA 92673.
www.sourcedmediabooks.com

Library of Congress Catalog Card Number: 2017934207
ISBN–13: 978-1-945431-08-1

Printed in the United States of America.

Dedication

We collectively dedicate this to Alice Gaye Christiansen, our beautiful, kind mother and wife. We love you, Mom. You are the glue that keeps all of our insanity from turning insane.

Contents

Introduction

This generation of teenagers is smarter, kinder, and better equipped to manage the problems and challenges of this crazy world than most adults are. In this book, we offer an opposing view to the nonsense that is broadly circulated regarding our next generation. We believe one hundred percent that many from this rising generation will astonish us.

This book was supposed to be a fun, quick three-month project, but it grew into a large, memorable experience that has given us much personal satisfaction. It has allowed us to have an amazing ongoing discussion about all of the important teen-parent topics through the formative teen years (Tim, age 15–17, and Alex, age 12–14). It has been an opportunity for us to work together and have deep-dive discussions not only as a family but also with many of the teenagers that hang out at our home. No topic or conversation has been left unturned. We have truly eaten our own cooking.

In this book, we (Tim and Rich) will be tag-teaming the chapters. At the end of each story, Alex, who is fourteen years old, will share his "Alex's Actions," or key takeaways that can immediately be applied to the learned concept.

Meet my sons, Tim and Alex.

Tim is our fun, bright, happy child—not only in personality, but he literally loves yellow. His room is bright yellow, his shoes are bright yellow, his hair is yellow, and until the age of 14, he refused to wear any other color of shirt. Although Tim is lively and enthusiastic, he also has one of the deepest and most tender souls I have ever encountered. He is such a hard worker and a profoundly spiritually grounded young man. He is a straight-A student, a loyal friend, and someone to whom I gravitate as a moral and purpose focus.

We jokingly say that Alex has all of our family IQ crammed into one brain. At the age of eight, Alex would regularly beat his older brothers, mom, and dad in family board games. Alex is easy to be around, a peacemaker, and has a crazy, sarcastic sense of humor. He is a hard worker and creates a calming influence on everyone he is around. I love to be with this young man.

Tim, Alex, and I love to shoot our compound bows together, climb mountains together, and go on travel adventures together. We work, play, and stay together. Tim and Alex are truly two of my favorite people in the world to hang out with.

Meet our dad, Rich.

My dad is either completely bongos, or he is an insane genius. He works hard, plays hard, and dreams hard. There is no such thing as an average day with him around. I just love going on adventures and hanging out with my dad. He is a very successful entrepreneur, chef, author, leader, and mentor. But, I think that his greatest accomplishments are in his family life. He has raised five successful sons, the fourth being myself. He has a couple of grandkids. And he has probably the most wonderful wife (and, in my case, mother) that he could possibly find. My dad may be successful, but that does not matter to me. What is more important to me is that I know he loves me, and I can count on him.

In this book, we will take turns sharing value-based stories that have fun and vibrant metaphors, as well as powerful learning opportunities. These stories will also respond to three recurring questions that Rich is often asked as he lectures around the world. These questions are:

1. How have you helped your teenage sons build five success-ful—and profitable—businesses?

2. Is it true that you do not pay for your sons' college tuition, service missions, or family vacations and, instead, help them create their own business in order to take accountability and fund these goals themselves?

3. What are the models, practices, and crazy things your family does as part of raising your children?

This book is not a detailed biography of our family. Instead, we pull from personal experiences and lessons we have learned. These stories are based on actual experiences, although names, places, and some details are changed to protect the innocent—or guilty, as the case may be.

In *chapter one*, we discuss the importance of unconditional love and the effects that this love can have upon children. This is the foundation upon which all parenting should be built and the reason that we named the book "Even if your toes turn purple."

In *chapter two*, we talk about how to set the stage and provide the environment for building good relationships. Get to know every family member, and spend quality time with each of them.

Chapter three is all about creating family traditions and bond-ing moments that last a lifetime.

Chapter four discusses helping kids learn through their trials. Even though it's never easy for parents to watch their children struggle, trials can be significant character-building experiences.

In *chapter five*, we talk about how important it is to keep promises to your kids. This trust is another foundational principle upon which good relationships form.

In *chapter six*, we discuss how to help your kids set goals and achieve them, even if the goals are "chicken chasing."

In *chapter seven*, we talk about how children can learn to be navigators and leaders on the sea of life. These leadership principles will help them throughout their entire lives.

In *chapter eight*, we discuss expectations and the importance of keeping high standards for your kids—and helping them achieve those standards.

In *chapter nine*, we outline strategies and techniques for strengthening the family unit and promoting family values.

In *chapter ten*, we explain the benefits of building a strong moral compass and letting that compass guide your actions.

In *chapter eleven*, we discuss the value of a dollar and the benefits of learning sound financial management practices.

In *chapter twelve*, we discuss ways to help your family develop an entrepreneurial mindset. We then delve into how to use that mindset to achieve financial stability.

In *chapter thirteen*, we focus on how to spread kindness and love and how to support those who need us most.

In *chapter fourteen*, we explore how to cultivate a strong work ethic and parlay it into a lifetime of success.

In *chapter fifteen*, we look at how to combat bullying and deal with the bullies in our lives.

In *chapter sixteen*, we explain how to develop compassion and understanding by learning from and emulating others.

In *chapter seventeen*, we explore how to talk to our children about the "hard topics"—like sex and pornography—early in life.

In *chapter eighteen*, we share ideas for maintaining balance and managing proper perspective, even when you are overwhelmed. We also discuss tactics for what to do if you feel like you're behind and struggling with your relationships with your children.

In ***chapter nineteen***, we call on the teenage generation to keep making the world a better place and to solve challenges that the generation before them couldn't.

In ***chapter twenty***, we conclude by reiterating our unwavering faith in teenagers and our desire to celebrate and find inspiration in their stories.

Enjoy the ride with the three of us as we share *Even If Your Toes Turn Purple.*

C h a p t e r   1

Even If Your Toes Turn Purple

b y   R i c h

Love unconditionally.

A muffled surge of electricity buzzed in the background. The neon sign flashed hues of washed-out yellow and vibrant purple through the crack in Tyler's curtains.

The muted sound of cars from the street subconsciously told Tyler that a new blanket of snow had covered the main street outside the "rat-trap" motel where he was staying.

A couch spring jabbed Tyler, gradually pulling him from a restless sleep. The musty stench of alcohol and stale smoke lingered through the room.

A splitting headache forced him into consciousness as he stumbled across the floor, making his way to the bathroom. A few steps into his journey, he tripped over one of the party guests who had crashed on the floor earlier that night. *What I wouldn't give for ten minutes of privacy and dudes not stealing my stuff,* he thought.

In a dull stupor, he reached for the sink and splashed water on his face. It was the closest he had come to a bath in nineteen days, and he desperately needed one after a night of getting wasted on dope and alcohol with his friends.

"Ugh," Tyler sighed. His so-called friends had used his last 23 dollars to buy the booze. No food, no job, no money, and nowhere to go. "What am I going to do?" he asked himself.

He looked at his reflection, seeing his signature black, unkempt hair and bloodshot eyes, which were dulled from a year of hard living. He glanced down at the jagged, asymmetrical tattoo on his left shoulder—a gift from a drunken friend. "Man, what a mess I've become," he mumbled.

Looking directly into the mirror, he couldn't help but ask himself, "How did I get here?"

Insistent, muffled cicada chirps filled the air. The night sky blanketed Ben's room with overtones of gray and washed-out brown. The final sliver of a waning moon gave him a glimpse of his roommate, Manzio, sleeping six feet away.

The musty smell of burnt coconut husks drenched the air of the village. The worn-out couch jabbed a broken coil into his left shoulder blade. He began to move toward consciousness as he became aware of an incessant, pounding headache.

When an overwhelming urge to vomit hit him, Ben surged fully into reality. As he maneuvered around Manzio, he tripped and broke his companion's peaceful slumber.

"Sorry, man," he mumbled, knowing their genuine friendship would earn him quick forgiveness. A few steps later, he heard several rats scurry under the stove. "Darn. Looks like it's time to go rat hunting again."

He wove through the two-room hut to the outside door, just in time to upchuck his entire dinner from the night before. One of the families that Ben was serving in Mozambique had offered their finest *xima and fish* as a gesture of friendship. Despite knowing sickness was a possible outcome, Ben and Manzio had graciously accepted and choked the fish heads down with a smile.

Back inside, Ben reached for the light switch, flipping it on. Nothing. "Another typical day," he mused as he reached for the matches—he knew right where to reach in the cupboard. After several strikes, a flame flickered to life, and he lit the nearly spent, yellow-wicked candle. He carefully dabbed a bit of precious, filtered water on a washcloth and then to his face. It was the closest Ben had come to a full shower in over five weeks.

By the flickers of light, Ben looked directly in the mirror. Reflected back were his bloodshot eyes and a face emaciated from shedding seventeen pounds in six weeks due to malaria. He couldn't help but ask himself, "How did I get here?"

In Tyler's dazed condition, the mirror seemed to answer him. His mind wandered back fifteen years.

The memory that came to him was that of being a confused, lanky three-year-old, looking into his mother's bloodshot eyes. Even at that age, he knew their life was hard. New men constantly came and went in their run-down apartment, and booze and drugs were a constant presence. Sometimes they ate, and sometimes he was left in his crib to cry, not knowing when his mother would be alert enough to take care of him and his older brother, Jacob. On this day, she walked briskly and refused to even glance at him. He couldn't quite understand why she was crying. They entered a pale, institutional-looking room. His mother gave him a quick kiss on the head and then quickly turned and left. Something had dramatically changed, and, in time, he came to understand that his mother had abandoned her two sons.

When he was given up for adoption, he didn't understand his vulnerable and weak feelings. All he could hope for was that someone would love him and that he might find some stability.

He remembered being delighted when, months later, his new parents-to-be walked into the room. His new mother was petite and beautiful, his new father handsome and grinning. He met his two smiling sisters and two older brothers. He imagined constancy in this new life, with regular meals to eat and no continual comings and goings like those of his drug-addicted mother.

He was relieved that Jacob was going to this new family too. His big, strong, adorable older brother had been his one source of stability. He knew, from what everyone said, that Jacob was only his half-brother, but that really didn't matter. Jacob was his hero, the one person he could always count on.

Although his new family seemed so good and happy on the outside, he was deeply troubled when he first heard his new mother calling him a "hard," "difficult," and "troubled" child. She always followed the declaration with a less-than-private whisper that she and her husband suspected Tyler would most likely end up like his birth mother, homeless and on drugs, or that they thought he had fetal alcohol syndrome and might not ever be "normal." Her comments didn't square with Tyler's initial belief that they would love him.

Tyler acted as most silly young boys do. He got dirty and wrestled continually with Jacob. He snuck food into his room, ensuring he'd have enough to eat, but his food stashes only sharpened his new mother's comments. He really did want to please her, but he had no idea how.

Tyler loved to build things and work with his hands; but no matter what he

> *He really did want to please her, but he had no idea how.*

did, he seemed to disappoint. He would take his bike apart only to find the brakes no longer worked; and, boy, did his parents let everyone know he'd messed up. They told him frequently that he was a failure, and he started to believe he was.

His mother moved him from school to school, always introducing him as a troubled kid with a learning disability or bipolar disorder or something. When he found a new friend, his mother went to the new friend's mother and warned her Tyler was a problem child. He wanted to be part of the "good kids" group; but when he started to go to their houses, he would be grounded for not doing chores or told he had five minutes to play. Who could play anything in five minutes?

Tyler knew he frustrated his parents a lot, especially his mother. He wondered why they had adopted him in the first place. He became troublesome in school, and his mom had to continually ride him about his grades. He wanted to excel, but he didn't fully understand how to "do better," and no advice was forthcoming. Looking at it now, his behavior was his plea to actually be recognized and acknowledged.

Looking at it now, his behavior was his plea to actually be recognized and acknowledged.

The other children in the family were biological; and, in hindsight, he realized they were treated very differently. When they went school shopping, the other children went to the mall and received whatever they needed to buy clothes. Jacob and Tyler were sent to the thrift store and told to pick out what they needed. Tyler was hard on clothes and started to enjoy drawing on himself, which drove everyone crazy. He realized it wasn't cool—but at least he was getting attention.

Because he had been told his entire life that he was a troublesome child, he started to take a bit of pride in being the "bad boy." He knew that if he acted out in school and he got in trouble, then at least someone was noticing him. The closest thing to love that he found was knowing someone cared enough to get mad at him.

Everyone in his neighborhood was kind and caring, yet no one seemed to notice that he was sinking. The police were called on him because he took a pencil out of his mom's purse (or because of some other crime he didn't commit), but even the police didn't notice the locks on his door. Locked out of the rest of the house, locked away from even the bathroom. Why did no one notice that his perfect-looking parents were emotionally abusing him? Why did no one do anything? Maybe, he thought, he really was worthless and unnoticeable.

As parents, our role modeling is our most basic responsibility. "We are handling life's scripts for our children," wrote Dr. Stephen R. Covey in his book *The 7 Habits of Highly Effective Families.* "These are scripts that, in all likelihood, will be acted out for much of the rest of their lives." He adds, "How important it is for us to realize that our day-to-day modeling is far and away our highest form of influence in our children's lives" (pg. 328).

Ben flashed back to *his* first childhood memory. He remembered sitting on the kitchen floor and banging his head over and over on the hardwood surface. He wailed and cried in hopes that he would be rewarded with the treat he needed *right then*. His deeply concerned mother rushed to him, picked him up off the floor, and hugged him. "Ben," she told him gently, "we love you; but banging your head on the floor is not the way to get what you want."

She had asked the pediatrician about his head-banging outbursts the previous week, and the doctor had just chuckled and said, "He is a little child with a strong personality. Banging his head on the floor is self-limiting, and he'll get over it."

With this information in mind, his father came into the kitchen, plucked him out of his mother's arms, and took him to timeout. Sitting together in timeout, his father looked at his darling boy with deep dimples and wide, sparkly brown eyes and said, "Ben, I love you. I'll love you forever. I would love you even if your toes were purple or if your hair turned green. I will even love you if your nose turns bright yellow. You are such an important part of this family; however, there are rules, and you have to be responsible. I expect more out of you than banging your head on the floor."

The sentiment of that day carried forward a few years, to a time when neighborhood bullies teased and mocked him. Ben had been a chubby little boy, and the bullies loved that. He came home crying one day, but his parents neither lectured nor spoke. His mother and father simply sat on either side of him, held him, and hugged him. He was safe and unconditionally loved. No matter how awkward and painful the bullying became, he never felt unsafe or unloved at home.

> *No matter how awkward and painful the bullying became, he never felt unsafe or unloved at home.*

Each night as his parents tucked him into bed, he stared up at the room and looked at the Winnie the Pooh painted on the wall. His father would read him his favorite nursery rhymes and then, with a smile on his face, would repeat those same soothing words: "I will love you forever. I will love you even if your toes turn purple or if your hair turns green. I will even love you if your nose turns bright yellow."

"I will love you forever. I will love you even if your toes turn purple or if your hair turns green. I will even love you if your nose turns bright yellow."

His father then extended his hands several inches and asked, "Do I love you this much?"

"No," Ben replied.

One foot apart. "This much?"

"No!"

His father then extended his arms as wide as he could and said, "I love you more than this." Ben smiled as his father would say, "Ben, you will always be loved."

As thirteen-year-old boys, Tyler and Ben had spent their summer together at scout camp, swamping canoes, sneaking out of their tents to throw pinecones at the leaders' tents, and sharing bone-chilling ghost stories.

Tyler later reflected on that summer, saying, "I wish I could go back and take the path Ben took. I wish we could have stayed friends." He looked to where their lives had taken separate routes. Ben had chosen good friends; he'd paid attention to his grades and to other important details in his life; he'd attempted to serve other people. Tyler recalled very specifically how Ben told him, "Tyler, you can do better than this." At the time, that had just made him mad, and he'd pulled away. Now he realized Ben had been right.

Ben also thought about Tyler, saying, "I wish he could come back and change the course of his life. If Tyler could have felt love, learned to serve others, and had just a little discipline," Ben mumbled, "life would have turned out a lot different for him."

He remembered asking about what happened at Tyler's house, with the calls to the police and the padlock on the fridge. Ben couldn't understand the strict rules at Tyler's house, knowing he was always welcome to help himself to the fridge at his own house.

In fact, sneaking treats from his mom's secret stash was a fun game he played with her. In his house, there were actually very few rules, but the expectations were high. The ultimate failure, in Ben's view, was disappointing his parents. Even so, it wasn't fear that motivated Ben but confidence that he could live up to his parents' expectations and his own potential. His parents had left no doubt about how high he could reach.

In contrast, Tyler had telegraphed to the world that he thought he would lose. He expected his life to be full of trials, and it was.

"We like to think of childhood as an idyllic time free of the burdens of responsibility that descend upon us with age," wrote human behavior expert and author Martin E. P. Seligman, Ph.D. "But, there is no shelter from pessimism and its grim offspring, depression. Many children suffer terribly from pessimism, a condition that torments them through the years to come, ruining their education and livelihoods, spoiling their happiness" (pg. 235).

Tyler's breaking point came when his parents threw Jacob out of the house. Jacob was his hero—a strong, charismatic, and funny young man who was preparing to spend his first two years out of high school volunteering to help others. However, their adopted parents discovered that Jacob had viewed some pornographic pictures on his video game system, a challenge that most young men have to learn to deal with. But instead of helping Jacob leave the porn behind, they declared him an addict to the whole neighborhood, vowed to warn away any girl he ever tried to date, and kicked him out of the house immediately. Their philosophy was clear: once a kid they had chosen to adopt turned eighteen, their job was done.

When Tyler saw that even Jacob couldn't be enough in that household—a kid who could have played college football on any team in the country and who had great grades—he knew all hope for him was gone. He stopped trying and began to rebel in earnest against his parents' strict rules and unreachable expectations. He quit going to school and, instead, rode his skateboard all around the neighborhood, acting the punk role his parents had defined for him. His life at home got disastrously worse with a padlocked fridge, a sealed bedroom door, and having to knock to be allowed in his "home."

Tyler turned to the only friends he thought would accept him. They were scoundrels, and he knew they were, but they were also fun—and accepting of him. He began smoking and finding any way he could to defy his parents.

He had what he thought was freedom. Things got worse, though, culminating in such animosity between him and his parents that he finally left and was formally thrown out of the house. Although his parents paid his rent, they made it very clear that any other help would stop the minute he turned eighteen years old. This terrified Tyler because he knew he didn't have the skills to cope in real life. So he smothered his pain with drugs and smoked pot as his one escape from the emotional pain.

A school counselor tried to help him. Tyler only needed a few credits to receive his high school diploma. A church leader helped him seek therapy; however, during the months-long climb out of his problems, he repeatedly crashed, undoing his progress. He decided he was just as self-destructive as his adoptive parents thought he was.

He even tried reaching out to his biological mother, but she wanted nothing to do with him. Everyone who should have loved him didn't.

> *Everyone who should have loved him didn't.*

Back in their respective dingy living conditions, both young men turned their thoughts to the future. For Tyler, the landscape was bleak. He had no idea how to move forward. Tyler stumbled, by the light of flashing neon, through the stale smoke, back to his lumpy couch. *I can't deal with this,* he thought, as he pulled a rancid blanket over his head, retreating to his only escape—sleep.

Ben, with the taste of vomit still in his mouth and the malaria still in his blood, thought, "I have capacity, I'm loved, and I'm safe. I have the courage to face this. I have a purpose." He put a smile on his face, and the electricity flickered on. He nudged Manzio awake—on purpose this time—and said, "Let's go make a real difference today."

Covey, Stephen R. *The 7 Habits of Highly Effective Families.* New York: Golden Books, 1997.

Seligman, Martin E. P. *Learned Optimism: How to Change Your Mind and Your Life.* New York: Vintage Books, 2006.

ALEX'S ACTIONS

It is important for parents to love their children unconditionally. They must let their children be responsible for the consequences of their actions, but they also need to love them, no matter what.

That can be hard when a child messes up, but that's when we need the most love. No kid really likes to be disciplined, but we know we need it sometimes. We just want to also feel like we're not a failure because we made a mistake!

- Teach your children about responsibility and consequences.

- At the same time, consistently remind them that they are loved.

- Remember: When a child messes up, that's when they need the most love.

- Our biggest limitation is the belief that when we make a mistake, we are not recoverable. The best gift you, as parents, can give us is unconditional love.

Chapter 2

Making It Epic

by Tim

Friends come and go, but families are forever.

"Sometimes the challenges you face are not in your own attitudes but in those of the people around you," wrote Ken Robinson in his book *Finding Your Element*. "Just because you're expected to achieve benchmarks in a certain way and by a certain time doesn't mean that this is the only path to follow" (pg. 163).

I was contemplative as I looked at the ridiculous and steep drop beneath me. One mistake could plunge me off Wayna Picchu to my resting place within the Incan valley. With that thought in my head, I clung to a vine ahead and I held on for support. Tightening my already bone-white grip, I thought, "My parents have definitely lost it this time!"

I grunted as I pulled myself up the final steps of the menacing stone-cut staircase and paused with awe, marveling at the lush green mountains I found myself facing. The moment was soon interrupted as my eyes fell on the next vile staircase. I let out a moan, then continued onward to the top of the peak.

Still traveling upward, I took a deep breath when I saw the final stretch to the summit. Then, looking down to where I had positioned my feet, I heard a menacing snap; and before I could realize what was happening, I plunged backward down the steep staircase. Another vine I had been holding onto as a lifeline had broken! Not wasting time to be graceful about it, I tumbled downward until someone caught me.

Before I could realize what was happening, I plunged backward down the steep staircase.

My body screamed at me, and my newfound bruises were like a packet of needles rattling in my skin. Once I got past the pain, I looked at the eyes staring back at me.

"Are you okay?" my dad asked.

"Good enough to finish this hike," I replied through gritted teeth. "You caught me?"

"Of course, Tim. I'm always here to catch you when you fall."

"Thanks, Dad." I paused. "You know what?"

"What?"

I grinned and said, "Our family sure knows how to make things epic!" And with that, my dad helped me up the rest of the mountain and set me on a rock to recover.

While sitting on a rock at the top of Wayna Picchu, gazing at one of the world's wonders, I couldn't help but think of all the amazing things my family had done. I thought of struggling up the cliffs of Nepal, swimming in the cool waters of the Amazon, our family road trips, and all of the other experiences I had lived in my short fourteen years. And then I considered how I had earned those experiences—all the struggles I'd faced to get there, the countless backbreaking tasks to earn the money, the intense hiking and training, preparing myself mentally to embrace the culture the world would throw at me. I've had to endure to truly live.

> *A family that stays together plays together.*

Then another thought hit me: My family was with me the whole time, from start to finish, from the preparation to being at a world wonder. A family that stays together plays together. We've had to work through thick and thin. We've conquered small and large tasks and obstacles—but because we support and help each other, there is nothing that we can't do as a family. We work together, we play together, we thrive together, and we grow together. And because we are together, we can make anything in life epic.

Robinson, Ken. *Finding Your Element*. New York: Penguin Books, 2013.

ALEX'S ACTIONS

A family that stays together plays together. If you want your family to be successful, happy, and united, get to know your family members, and spend quality time with them. Even when he was falling, Tim knew our dad was always there to help and support him because he had been there every time.

- Friends come and go, but family stays with you forever. Although friends and acquaintances are important, the people you will know the best and spend the most time with are your family members. So you need to love and support them.

- Life is too short not to do adventurous, epic things. When you find free or leisure time, use it wisely for your family's benefit. "Epic" may look different to different families, but epic family experiences—and all the preparation before and the reminiscing after—help build the family as a whole.

- Do all things in balance. Don't go spending thousands of dollars you don't have in hopes of making your life epic. Make sure you have the income and proper preparations before you do anything. The preparations and anticipation, when done as a family, can be as much a part of the epic experience as the event itself.

A NOTE FROM RICH

Why We Climb Mountains

My wife and I have deliberately used climbing mountains in our family as an opportunity to help our children prepare for life. We have found this to be a profound way to teach self-discipline, self-reliance, endurance, and patience. Our children have learned that they can do hard things and that hard things are worth doing.

While we are in the backcountry, we have the added benefit of unplugging from cell phones and other devices. This gives us uninterrupted time to have deep conversations, to really get to know each other while striving for a common goal. We encourage our children to participate in team sports or other group activities to learn teamwork, camaraderie, and sportsmanship. However, when it comes to finding who they are and reaching deep inside their gut to see if they have the strength to stick it out, there is no substitute for a long, hard-fought battle up a mountainside. It teaches our youth to value the private victory rather than the public victory. At the top of the mountain peak, there is not a crowd of fans cheering from the bleachers or cheerleaders waving their pom-poms in the air. The victory is the internal satisfaction and confidence that wells up inside, knowing that we can do hard things.

I am not attempting to convert everyone to start mountain climbing. What I am proposing is that you collaborate with your family to consciously and deliberately choose strengthening bonding activities to do together that afford your children the opportunity to learn perseverance, self-discipline, and how to win the private battles in life.

Chapter 3

Pirate Mountain Treasure

by Rich

Build family traditions.

Drip . . . drip . . . drip . . . fell beads of perspiration from the fat cheeks of the two young boys and little girl marching up a gentle canyon slope. On this hot July day, the towering pines seemed to reach for the sky, and the sun bathed the young children as they meandered after their father.

They followed a roughly cut dirt path that wasn't quite well worn enough to keep dandelions and sprigs of grass from attempting to overtake the cleared space. A spring running alongside the trail beckoned the three with its coolness, but they were not distracted.

"March, march, march, march, march, march, march, march." The words echoed through the small canyon as the children swung their arms to the cadence.

"Hi-ho, hi-ho, fiddly fo, a pirate's life, here we go!

The children were on a mission, which could be seen in their faces. Their eyes were cold and sharp like steel, and you could tell they were marching with purpose.

"March, march, march, march, march, march, march, march.

"We are brave, we are strong, we will fight evil all day long.

"March, march, march, march, march, march, march, march."

The children were on a mission, which could be seen in their faces. Their eyes were cold and sharp like steel, and you could tell they were marching with purpose. Their father—a man in his early 30s who bore a sly grin and a shovel—led the cadence. Beads of sweat also slid down his face.

It soon became evident that their destination was a short way ahead, so they pressed on, chanting and marching, although it didn't make much sense to be singing or telling stories of pirates. The determined father and children were 10,000 feet above sea level, surrounded by quaking aspens and tall pines, with the occasional deer or squirrel darting through the brush. Of course, any animal was usually enough to interrupt the children's determined marching, which always brought them back to thoughts of pirates.

Whenever they stopped, their dad would say, "Watch out for the pirates!"

The older boy, who was about six, carried a brass chest under his arm. The little girl was carrying a locket half-in and half-out of her pocket. Upon arriving at a meadow, they stopped for some water and licorice. They had finally reached the right spot, and their

The determined father and children were 10,000 feet above sea level, surrounded by quaking aspens and tall pines, with the occasional deer or squirrel darting through the brush.

father proceeded to tell a tale—a scary tale of pirates who had once inhabited this very forest.

> *"This is where they buried their treasure, and it still lies in these very woods. As they did with their treasure, so shall we with ours."*

About 200 years ago, old Silver Tongue, the great pirate of the Caribbean, became tired of the heat and humidity and decided to take his crew to summer in the mountains. The children didn't know what "summer" meant when used as a verb, but it sounded impressive.

"So," their father said, "this great pirate marched his crew all the way from the ocean up into the mountains, and they found this very spot, right where the three of us stand now, and made this their retreat.

"This is where they buried their treasure, and it still lies in these very woods. As they did with their treasure, so shall we with ours. You see, these are magical woods. If we deposit our treasure here carefully and strategically, then through the winter, the pirates' treasure will magically gather to our treasure."

The little girl's eyes were as big as saucers; she jumped as a deer scurried behind a bush while both boys waited expectantly for Silver Tongue's pirates to emerge holding pistols and cutlasses.

After the story, the children took a string and tied it at the bases of four chosen trees, creating a crisscross. At the center of the X, they dug a hole for their treasure.

Opening the football-sized treasure chest, the father couldn't help but chuckle. He had invited his children to put two or three of their most precious possessions inside. The trove included several Pokémon cards, a princess toy, a sticker from a quarter machine, and an assortment of coins, including a precious buffalo nickel. But the personal favorite of the two boys—and to the disgust of the little girl—was a grasshopper they had caught the day before and wrapped neatly in a plastic bag.

The children watched in wonder as the hole got deeper, each taking a turn using the shovel. The younger boy was invited to secure the lock on the chest. Then they placed the chest in two plastic bags and solemnly delivered it into the earth. The ceremony culminated in the children shoveling dirt over the top, reassembling the sod, and taking down the crude X that marked the hidden spot.

When their work was done, the children sat down on the spot, and their father shared another story, this one about more than mere pirate gold and crazy Silver Tongue the pirate.

He said, "This is a very important spot to me and to you. You see, your mother brought me here to this very meadow and this same exact spot for my birthday lunch when we were falling in love; and here she gave me a wonderful kiss. As a matter of fact, this tiny meadow is where I presented your mother *her* treasure, the sign and token of my love: her engagement ring. You see, this is the place where I proposed to your mother."

The children's eyes widened and brightened, not out of the fear of pirates summering in an enchanted forest, but out of calm, out of the sure feeling born out of the deep love their father had for their mother. They felt stable and strong.

But soon the children grew restless, and the father said, "Come on, I have one more treasure to show you."

They then hopped across the little brook and went to a modest grove of aspens.

After a few minutes of searching, the father found a tree with some words engraved into the bark. As the children got closer, they put their chubby hands on the carved lettering. The oldest boy, to his great delight, realized what it was.

His father's initials were carved in the tree. Under those was the word "loves," followed by his mother's name.

His father's initials were carved in the tree. Under those was the word "loves," followed by his mother's name.

"Children," their dad said, "on that very day, I fell in love with your mother. We came down to this aspen and carved our initials into the tree together. And here, some fifteen years later, the exact tree still grows."

The kids laughed and said, "Sheesh, Dad."

Then with great glory and dignity, the pirate adventure ended as the father and his children marched down the beautiful little canyon (this time not sweating so much, what with gravity on their side). The brook still babbled along their path, the grass was still green and lush, and the flowers still reached for the sun. The kids felt happy, alive, peaceful, vibrant, and full of adventure.

The following year, on an overcast July day with interspersed light and sprinkling rain, their father again threw a shovel over his shoulder, and he and his three children began their march back to the meadow.

"March, march, march, march, march, march, march, march.

"Hi-ho, hi-ho, fiddly fo, a pirate's life is here to go!

"March, march, march, march, march, march, march, march.

"We are brave, we are strong, we will fight evil all day long.

"March, march, march, march, march, march, march, march."

They progressed through the canyon, finally reaching their secret, sacred spot. The oldest boy wrapped some string across the same trees as the year before, and, together with his brother and little sister, dug up their treasure.

The calm and peace the oldest boy gained from this grounding experience was as great as the elation he had felt upon finding his buried treasure.

When they reached the chest, their father leapt forward and shouted, "Quick! Pirates! Hide!"

The children dashed for the trees, and the father pulled something from out of his pocket. His children returned eventually, and after soothing their nerves for a bit, he tugged the brass treasure chest out of the ground. Carefully, they lifted the latch and found true treasure awaiting them. There were strange coins, little jewels, and all sorts of new, small treasures that had appeared, taken from the pirates' lost horde. The moment evoked magic in every way, and the children jumped and danced with glee.

Then the prized grasshopper flopped out from the jewels. Yes, it was rotten and stinky. At least it hadn't attracted any other dead grasshoppers.

After separating the bug from their bounty, the kids asked, "Dad, can we please go down and see the tree?"

They walked down to the little creek and jumped across it. Once the oldest son found the aspen, he outlined the engraved letters with a careful finger. The calm and peace the oldest boy gained from this grounding experience was as great as the elation he had felt upon finding his buried treasure.

If one analyzes this experience, it's hard not to laugh. The ocean is some 2,000 miles away. Why would pirates carry their treasure across 2,000 miles of mountains and rivers just to "summer" in an enchanted forest?

But what should be learned is that the father was creating traditions. Amy Griswold, former educator of family life at the University of Illinois Extension, wrote, "Traditions give security to young people, providing a sense of continuity and routine that they can depend on year after year. Such activities help promote healthy relationships between the generations when they are enjoyed and anticipated by everyone."

The father was creating stories, and he was creating symbols and grounding points for his children. These treasure-hunting trips became some of the strongest, happiest, and most peaceful memories of these children's lives and are something they still talk about.

Families become unified and have great joy when they combine stories with beliefs, create symbols (things we can see that remind us of key ways of being), and establish rituals (events or things we do repeatedly that open our minds to new ways of thinking) in their adventures.

I'm sure, at the time, that this father did not consciously plot to hit all three points. It probably just felt right. But this grand adventure created a calm grounding and learning experience for his children that they will always remember.

Griswold, Amy. "Facts for Families." University of Illinois Extension (2016). Available at http://web.extension.illinois.edu/ccdms/facts/121204.html.

ALEX'S ACTIONS

I'm not old enough to be able to look back at family traditions and see their value. But I am smart enough to know how much I enjoy the traditions my parents have been creating for me and my brothers since I can remember. And I remember the little ones as well as the big ones, whether it's all sitting down for dinner together (when we're all home), going on an epic hike, or doing something for another family at Christmastime.

Check back with me in a few years, but I think I'll remember lots of these times together when I have kids of my own. And I already know I'll be creating traditions and rituals just for them! What my parents do is a huge part of what connects me to them, and I want to make sure my children feel exactly the same way.

- Build traditions. Whether it's sitting down for dinner, going on hikes, or doing service at Christmastime, traditions create shared memories that tie families together.

Chapter 4

The View from the Top

by Tim

"It's not the mountain we conquer, but ourselves."
–Sir Edmund Hillary

I went forward, wincing with every dreaded step. There was no way out of it. All I could do was keep going until what seemed to be my certain death.

The cool wind that tickled at my face was soon replaced by the trickling of sweat. I kept moving, fighting through the painful burn of each stride. As I pressed forward, my old pains were numbed, only to be replaced by new ones. As the throbbing in my body increased and fatigue grew, I fell to the ground and cried while sitting on a pile of dirt. My ten-year-old, undeveloped muscles ached too much for me to use them. I decided then that I would stay and never leave my

> *My ten-year-old, undeveloped muscles ached too much for me to use them.*

> *I knew that this was
> the best place I could
> wish for a peaceful,
> admirable death.*

pile of dirt, that I would stop trying. I would never make it up the cruel Namche Hill.

I looked at the beautiful Himalayan mountains that my family and I had been hiking throughout the summer, and I knew that this was the best place I could wish for a peaceful, admirable death.

My father, hiking just ahead, saw me planted in dirt and unwilling to move. He stopped and walked back to where I had fallen—he seemed only slightly irritated at retracing his steps.

"Tim," he said softly as he kneeled next to me.

"Yeah?" I muttered.

"So you don't think you'll make it?" He shifted to sit beside me. "You're giving up that easily?"

I hadn't thought of my decision as giving up until that moment. "I guess so," I replied, choking on my words.

"You know, Tim, this hill isn't going to get any smaller, and it will take you a while before you get any bigger. So you might as well just sit here until you die." My dad looked me right in the eyes. "Or you could hike this hill so you can conquer bigger ones when you are older. Just imagine the views you would see."

In an article for *Psychology Today* called "Overcoming Obstacles," Karyn Hall, Ph.D., explains that the ability to identify and overcome challenges relies on personal perspective. She writes, "Some people see obstacles as a puzzle to solve. Some see obstacles as an opportunity to grow. Others see obstacles as threats. Still others see obstacles as meaning they cannot succeed. Your view of barriers to achieving your goals affects how you react."

> *"Or you could hike
> this hill so you can
> conquer bigger ones
> when you are older.
> Just imagine the
> views you would see."*

This determination is what helped me move forward. Suddenly, my body found the strength it needed. I hiked the hill and continued on to the next without hesitation.

I learned a valuable lesson at that point in my ten-year-old life: If I give up at my lowest point, how will I ever be able to see the view from the top of the mountain?

Hall, Karyn. "Overcoming Obstacles." *Psychology Today* (2016). Available at https://www.psychologytoday.com/blog/pieces-mind/201605/overcoming-obstacles.

ALEX'S ACTIONS

When you feel like giving up, remember your destination and keep going, because your discouragement will go away only if you keep going. If you give into discouragement, you won't gain the strength and perseverance to conquer the next challenge.

- When you get discouraged, remember your destination and press on.

- Remember: We are on this earth to learn. If you are struggling with something, use it as an opportunity to learn, because it will probably be something you'll need to know later in life.

- When helping someone who has fallen or is discouraged, avoid using criticism. Rather, encourage him or her through kindness and love.

Chapter 5

Danny's Pokémon Christmas

b y R i c h

Keep your promises.

I was in a foul mood when we arrived at the crowdless Burger King, which was empty of customers aside from an excited little boy and an old lady who appeared to be in her mid 80s. The traffic that day had been terrible, and driving in the falling snow with young children was even worse.

In addition to the traffic, I was feeling picked on. I had just started a new job that required a commute through road construction and over icy roads for more than an hour each way. I wasn't even sure I liked this new job.

I had been traveling a lot and had promised my sons I would take them to Burger King to buy a Pokémon meal and trading cards as a feeble attempt to compensate for my time away. That night was the only free evening I could make good on that promise to my precious boys—so storm or no storm, the drive had to happen.

We *loved* Pokémon trading; it was one of the things we did together. Pikachu, Blastoise, Charizard, Articuno . . . they were characters that bridged the gap between me—a tired, young father—and my energetic young sons. When I traveled, I tried to find them cards they couldn't easily find, giving us all something to look forward to when I returned home.

On this particular night, Burger King was putting a limited-edition Pokémon toy and a Poké Ball in each kid's meal. The boys had been anticipating the outing from the minute they heard about the collector toys.

> *We learned that his name was Danny, and he was collecting Pokémon toys too.*

With cold feet and eager eyes, the boys ordered and took their bagged meals to the table to sit down when they noticed a skinny, straggly little boy that had to be around eight years old. He had unkempt hair, and his toes stuck out from a large hole at the end of his shoes—and he was eagerly watching to see which toys were in my boys' meals.

After he had watched my boys with sparkling eyes and anticipation, he hesitantly approached us to check out our prizes. As we all started to chat, we learned that his name was Danny, and he was collecting Pokémon toys too. Pokémon were his favorite thing, like they were for many eight-year-olds at the time.

When my boys opened their toys, each one received a treasured Pokémon. My son Matthew happened to get one of the really good ones: a Raichu. Everyone oohed and aahed at Matthew's rare and valued toy. Danny, obviously wanting the Raichu, very politely and thoughtfully negotiated for it, knowing that part of the fun of Pokémon was trading to get better, more powerful ones. Danny's varied and earnest efforts were of no avail, because Matthew declined to part with it.

After our meal, we got in our car and began to drive away. As we were pulling out of the parking lot, we saw Danny and the old lady with him hobbling along in the snow. My wife felt impressed to pull back and ask if they needed a ride. They gladly accepted. As they got into the car, the story unfolded.

Danny's great-grandmother was raising him after raising three children of her own and three grandchildren. Danny's mother had abused and neglected him for the first year and a half of his life. She had been strung out on drugs and served time in prison. He had a 20-year-old aunt whom he loved and idolized. She was now in college and attempting to get through as quickly as possible so she could adopt him. The great-grandmother was concerned she might die before the aunt was old enough to become Danny's legal guardian.

They had no car, and the great-grandmother had suffered from a fall and was left with a broken hip and injured shoulder. She wore worn-out canvas tennis shoes, soaked through from walking in the deep snow. But Danny lived for Pokémon, so the two of them had walked from the west side of town, in the snow, to go to Pokémon Trading Night at Burger King.

During the drive, Danny shared his excitement about going home for Christmas to see his mom for the first time in four years. I noticed the worried look in his sweet great-grandmother's face. I think we were both concerned that the boy was being set up for a huge disappointment.

When we pulled into their humble driveway and let them out of our warm, comfortable car, tears welled in my eyes, and my heart broke. What chance did Danny have? By contrast, how decadent and indulgent were we? How blessed were we? Every member of our family loved each other and put the others first!

The two of them had walked from the west side of town, in the snow, to go to Pokémon Trading Night at Burger King.

Although it was very hard for my three young sons, Matthew, John,

> *"I wish I was magic. I would wave my arms, make me another Raichu Poké Ball, and make that little boy's mom and dad love him."*

and Nathan said their goodbyes by independently giving Danny their Poké Balls. Matthew, especially, had a big tear in his eye as he parted with the treasured Raichu. But they each felt like they needed to give this boy a small gift at Christmas. When we returned home, Matthew said, "I wish I was magic. I would wave my arms, make me another Raichu Poké Ball, and make that little boy's mom and dad love him."

I am not sure that Danny remembers my boys, but I know that my boys will always remember Danny. We do not know what happened to Danny. We do not know what trajectory his life took. What I do know is that God loves Danny as he loves each of us, and we all need to be more conscious and self-aware so we can serve each other. I also know that confidence, self-worth, and joy come from helping and serving others.

Each year at Christmastime, our family lights candles and talks about something we are grateful for. Robert Emmons, professor of psychology at UC Davis, wrote, "Gratitude is more than a pleasant feeling; it is also motivating. Gratitude serves as a key link between receiving and giving: It moves recipients to share and increase the very good they have received." Every year since meeting Danny, at least one of my sons brings up his name and the feelings he had that night at Burger King.

ALEX'S ACTIONS

As parents, keep your promises to your children—especially if you must be physically absent or if there is instability in your family. Put forth the effort to invest time and energy in things that are important to them.

Sometimes we get so caught up in our own problems that we forget other people's trials and emotions. Make sure you try to recognize other people and help them—it will make their journey and yours better.

- Keep your promises to your children.

- Take the time to look at all you have: your friends, family, personal belongings, and other things that are significant to you. Think about how different your life would be without them, and gratitude should come easily.

- Do good. Simple acts of kindness can go a long way. Knowing they are cared for and thought of can lift another person—and yourself.

Chapter 6

Chicken Chasing

by Tim

Set SMART goals.

"Ugh," I moaned as I waited for my mother in the car. As an eleven-year-old boy, I didn't have the patience for this.

The tinted window restricted my contact with the bright morning light. The car that enclosed me was the only thing keeping me from running and basking in the warmth of the sun. My thoughts continued for a minute more until something caught my eye: a pompous chicken flaunting its tail feathers down the middle of the road!

My leg twitched with impatience. The sapphire sky called for me. I knew that if I didn't examine the chicken further, I wouldn't have any adventure on such a great day.

My gaze returned to the chicken. It seemed to stare straight into my soul. It gave me the same look of curiosity that I probably returned.

Then, out of the blue, it mocked me, branding me boring, by breaking its gaze.

I debated what to do. My mother had told me to wait in the car until she was done getting the mail. On the other hand, six months ago, my family had set New Year's goals. While my family members picked serious goals —"get my driver's license," "go on a family vacation," "earn money," and so forth—I had a stroke of brilliance. Once it was my turn to write down a new family goal, I smirked at my genius and wrote "Chicken chasing."

I knew this opportunity at the post office was one I couldn't miss. Living in the middle of a city, it isn't every day that you run into a chicken at the post office. I glared at the chicken, determined to achieve my goal, as it merrily plucked at the weeds in the road. My hands were sweating as I reached for the car handle.

All at once, the chase was on. I swung my door open and leaped for the chicken, who was now stretching out her feathers in the morning light.

The chicken was beyond surprised, and her eyes seemed to shrink into her brain when I grabbed her. She tried flapping and running wildly around, but I had a handhold on her fat leg, so her attempts were in vain—that is, until she started pecking at my hand.

Before long, I couldn't stand the pain and let go. And, with that, the chase was on once more! We ran zigzags through the post office bushes and circles around the parking lot.

About five minutes into my chase, my mother exited the post office and could only laugh as she saw me traumatize this poor chicken. Exhausted and tired, but filled with pleasure at fulfilling my pointless goal,

Once it was my turn to write down a new family goal, I smirked at my genius and wrote "Chicken chasing."

I decided it was time to say farewell to my chicken friend and head home with my mother.

"When you learn to take full responsibility for setting a goal, you'll reach it in no time," wrote Steve Chandler in his book *Reinventing Yourself.* "Absolute focus is the key to all great human achievement." He adds, "Taking ownership is the highest form of focus. It's a willingness to bring everything you've got to the situation. To live in the now. When you do that, your spirit wakes up to join you in the fun" (pg. 54).

That little act carved a lesson into my heart for eternity: It doesn't matter how small or stupid a goal is or how much or little it matters to you. What does matter is having the overwhelming joy of chasing the chickens in life.

Chandler, Steve. *Reinventing Yourself: How to Become the Person You've Always Wanted to Be.* Pompton Plains, NJ: The Career Press, Inc., 2005.

ALEX'S ACTIONS

Antoine de Saint-Exupéry said, "A goal without a plan is just a wish." Setting goals is great, but working hard to accomplish them is where you find the fun in goal setting.

Most goals are forgotten not long after they are set. When setting goals, don't just come up with them. Write them down, and think about them until you accomplish them.

When Tim chased the chicken, he didn't make a measly pass at it and call it good. He chased that chicken until they were both exhausted. When reaching for goals, don't put in the minimum effort. Try to reach your full potential.

When creating a goal, use this SMART acronym to make the goal as useful as possible.

- **S: Specific** – Make sure all details are included.

- **M: Measurable** – Create metrics by which you can measure success (time, amount, etc.). Even for abstract goals (for example, "make new friends"), you can create milestones (meet X number of new people, go to a new location every week, etc.).

- **A: Achievable** – Realistically assess whether the goal is possible for you. For example, if you've never run a race, don't set a goal to run a marathon in a month. Set smaller, more realistic goals that will get you closer to the big goal.

- **R: Relevant** – Set goals you have a reason to strive for! If your goals have no relevance to the person you want to become, it will be difficult to find the motivation to follow through, and the effort might take away from more important goals.

- **T: Time-Based** – Decide if the goal is short- or long-term, and give yourself deadlines.

Chapter 7

The Four People You Meet on the Sea of Life

by Rich

Navigate the sea of life.

It was my fourth encounter with the salty old seaman. The experiences of life had etched wrinkles and expression lines across his wise face. His whitewashed hair curled untamed around his ears and wildly poked out from beneath his flat cap.

Captain Roy was not your typical crusty, crass captain. Indeed, he was a Chancellor, an Admiral, the Wizard, the Master of his Domain. His steely blue eyes cut through you like a hot knife. Everyone timidly approached him, knowing his sharp words could slice you quicker than a street fighter's dagger. I saw him that day on top of his tower, arm resting against the helm, pointing his way north. People had come from far and wide to seek wisdom from this seafaring man, for he had experience that even nobles and the most learned sought after.

You can always tell Drifters by the distant look in their eyes; they seem a bit whipped, and life has control of them.

As he sat on his tower, perched on the throne, his shoulders back and his long pointy finger waggling in the direction of anyone who dared challenge him, he profoundly spoke of the Navigator.

"You'll meet four people upon the seas of life!" he exclaimed. "You meet them over and over and over again. No matter how you try to invent new ones, these same characters will always show up.

"The first that you will find upon your journeys are the Drifters—they make up most of the seafaring population. They're tossed to and fro with the waves. They respond and react according to the storms that beset them, but they really don't act on life. You can always tell Drifters by the distant look in their eyes; they seem a bit whipped, and life has control of them. They will frequently make comments, such as, 'I'm working for the man,' or 'Whatever, sir,' and they just seem to float along, taking chances as they come, living paycheck to paycheck, going from circumstance to circumstance, and wandering through life. They feel they'll never get a break. They don't quite drown, but they also never quite reach their full potential."

He then looked directly at the woman to my right and asked, "Marie, are you a Drifter?"

In shock, she squirmed and said, "No, Roy, I don't want to be a Drifter."

His eyes lightened, intensity ceased. "Good, nor do I. Choosing not to be a Drifter is simply a matter of deciding not to be passive in your life."

He continued: "The second type of seafarers in the sea of life are the Surfers. The Surfers set their fixed points upon the water. They surf from wave to wave and have a really good time. They get to feel the thrill of going up and down, but they never go much farther than the beach they start out on. Surfers frequently confuse motion with momentum. They are charismatic, confident, and often appear successful. They might surf to wealth, power, prestige, high adventure, or just plain fun.

"Surfers will do their darndest to convince you they are focusing on durable and meaningful objectives and not in fact surfing. But if you peel back the motives and look to the end result of their efforts, the true story is told. I've met many captains in my day who were great Surfers. They made a great show of going from point to point, but they never accomplished anything of great meaning or gravity. They experienced the joy of each wave, but never got much beyond where they started.

Surfers will do their darndest to convince you they are focusing on durable and meaningful objectives and not in fact surfing.

"Now don't take me wrong," Captain Roy said, "we all like to surf and do fun, exciting things. However, if you set your sights upon unfixed objects, whether on land or sea, you will be deceived, and you will not reach the full potential of what you are meant to be. Surfers are a lot of fun, and oftentimes they do accomplish meaningful things. However, it is not deliberate, it is not with intention, and it is not true and marked leadership."

Captain Roy directed his gaze and his comments toward the fun-loving jokester in the group. "We all enjoy surfing from time to time don't we, Rob? Nothing wrong with it, but we all know there is more don't we?" Turning red and lowering his head, Rob shrugged, admitting that even *his* humor was not the end game.

"The third set of individuals that you encounter are indeed the dirty dogs, the most unpleasant of all we encounter. These are the Drowners.

"These unfortunate souls, no matter how hard they try, can't seem to get a break. One day you receive word from them that they are in trouble. You do your very best to bolster them and

> *The only person worse than a Drowner is the fool who enables the Drowner.*

keep them afloat, but somehow within a matter of a few weeks they manage to lose track of their lifelines. They're always drowning; they expect to lose. As a matter fact, they manufacture losing. These poor souls will try your patience. Sometimes you might feel like you want to just take their heads, dunk them under the water, and hold them there and tell them to 'just get it over with.'

"The only person worse than a Drowner is the fool who enables the Drowner. Often, this well-intentioned 'help' not only sends the Drowner deeper into the dark bowels of the ocean, but it also puts the poor fool attempting the rescue in danger of drowning too.

"I am not saying we should not help the Drowner, but for heaven's sake, don't jump in feet first with no life preserver and let him pull your head underwater. You have to prepare yourself with a life preserver and lifesaving skills before you can fully rescue someone else.

"That being said, there are times in every one of our lives that we may start to drown, and we would hope that there would be someone who would reach out and pull us back into the boat.

"So what are we to do with Drowners? This is a difficult question.

"Jesus Christ taught us that if there are 99 sheep in the flock, but one is lost, we are to go seek the one that is lost and return him to the fold. Furthermore, once he is found, we're not only to return him to the flock but also celebrate his return."

At this point, there was not one person who dared move or stir, for we knew that irrespective of religious differences in the group, Roy was teaching profound principles.

"Drowners are people, so they are important; and you should do what you can for them without endangering yourself or enabling their drowning habits. But you should always aim to be more than a Drowner yourself. You should aim to be a Navigator.

Navigators lead their lives with purpose.

"Navigators are the fourth and rarest people that you will find on the sea of life. Great captains who are Navigators will make a plan in order to get their ship, their crew, their passengers, and themselves to the desired destination safely. Navigators lead their lives with purpose. They may hit some storms along the way, but they know where they are going and what they want to do.

"Very few of us have the courage to be Navigators." Captain Roy's iron eyes pierced each participant in the crowd. "I choose to be a Navigator," he said.

"Are you a Navigator?" he asked. We all leaned forward, engaging, wanting to be Navigators.

"Navigators set their sights on one fixed object. You see, in this universe, there is only one stable point for a seafarer in the Northern Hemisphere: the North Star. All the other millions of stars in the sky move, but all sailors know the North Star is fixed. It is not on the land, so using it to navigate does not cause us to be tossed to and fro, following a moving target. The star is sometimes difficult to see because of the clouds and stormy weather; however, in every moment of calm, we fix our sights on the North Star and take our direction from it. Navigating by the North Star often requires that we cut against tides, that we go upstream, or that we sail into storms. Do you have the courage to sail into the storms in your life? Do you have courage to hack into the waves and the storms to accomplish meaningful goals?"

Captain Roy rested his hands on the helm. "You see, leadership and the course of the Navigator can be very lonely." He then recited another verse of scripture, emphasizing how alone Christ felt at times: "The foxes have holes and the birds of the air have nests, but the Son of Man has nowhere to lay His head" (Matthew 8:20). He continued, "Oftentimes Navigators have to fight through fear and pain in order to lead, despite not having all the answers themselves.

"Do you have the courage to do this?"

As we stood upon the sturdy bow atop of the ship's tower, we looked toward the North Star, and I firmly resolved that through the remainder of my life I would make every attempt to be a Navigator.

The average person will drown at least two or three times during his or her life.

This story, first told by Roy H. Williams, poignantly illustrates the power of perspective. What are you? Are you a Drifter? Are you a Surfer? Are you a Drowner? Or are you a Navigator?

Through the course of our lives, each one of us is each of those characters at different times. The average person will drown at least two or three times during his or her life. (This is yet another very important reason we need to be prepared and try to help the Drowners, because indeed each of us will have times when we need to be rescued.) However, each one of us also has many opportunities to be a Navigator if we take that chance.

As you fight the fierce winds and have the courage to navigate into the storms, there may be a time that you're swept off the bow, needing to be rescued. Do not apologize for it, but make sure to put your life preservers where they are readily available. When you once again have a solid deck beneath your feet, seek again to be a Navigator and to make a difference in this world.

ALEX'S ACTIONS

Sometimes even Navigators can't see the North Star. If you are unsure where you are headed, work as hard as you can to dispel the clouds blocking the North Star until it is visible again.

- Help the people in your life who are drowning, but don't let them take you down with them. Find a way to get them back to shore.

- Though it may be hard to get back on the ship, do all in your power to get there.

- Remember: Navigators are good at both leading and following.

Chapter 8

I Don't See What the Problem Is

by Tim

Develop stamina, and trust the process.

Brittany threw open the door to her house and slammed it behind her. She stomped her way to the front room, kicked off her shoes, and threw her purse to the ground. She rose a shaking fist to the heavens, exclaiming, "What have I done wrong?"

Brittany's dad listened patiently from the other room, waiting for Brittany to calm down. Once the initial signs of frustration passed, he went to her.

Brittany watched as her father entered the room. Her father had always seemed young, but he was aging now, growing duller, and his slicked-back hair was starting to gray. He wore his usual outfit—a neatly ironed dress shirt with a brown suit coat and a royal purple tie. Crow's feet crinkled around his eyelids, which veiled his blind, false eyes.

> *"Medical school is too hard. Everyone there is trying to kill me!"*

Brittany's father interrupted his daughter's thoughts with his loving yet firm lawyer voice: "I thought that you were up at the university. What are you doing three hours from campus?"

Brittany thought for a moment, then said, "Dad, I came down for the weekend. Medical school is too hard. Everyone there is trying to kill me! I can't do anything right, my grades are falling, and I just can't take anymore. The teachers give us material that's impossible to understand, and I'm not even sure it will be worth it! If I can make it through."

Brittany's father drew a deep breath, then said calmly, "Do you have the books to study?"

"Yes, but—"

Her father cut her off. "Do you have the transportation to get to the places you need to be?"

"Yeah, I guess I do."

"Do you have the right tools and education to get good grades?"

"Of course, Dad, but it is . . ." Brittany rambled until she saw her father's point. She was arguing with a blind man who studied for six years to be a lawyer. He'd had to get a tutor to follow him to almost all of his classes to read the material for him; he'd had no transportation besides his quick walks on a campus that required sight for safety.

Brittany suddenly realized how hard her father's college experience must have been. Brittany was complaining, when she had every advantage. Her father had made it through law school, having to memorize the material after hearing it only once.

Brittany had no argument and could only mutter, "But . . ."

> *She was arguing with a blind man who studied for six years to be a lawyer.*

"Brittany, you may say it is hard, but I just don't see what the problem is."

When we have set our goals into place, it's important to trust the process needed to achieve them without compromising what is important. In their book, *Living Forward: A Proven Plan to Stop Drifting and Get the Life You Want,* authors Michael Hyatt and Daniel Harkavy warn us that the path isn't always predictable. "Maybe you'll start out with a burst of energy, get stuck, and want to quit," they state. "That sometimes happens. Don't despair. Keep your head in the game." Or, maybe it's the opposite. In that case, Hyatt and Harkavy say, "If you arrive distracted or discouraged and have a difficult time getting started, the same advice holds. Don't despair. Trust the process" (pg. 113).

Hyatt, Michael, and Daniel Harkavy. *Living Forward: A Proven Plan to Stop Drifting and Get The Life You Want.* Grand Rapids, MI: Baker Books, 2016.

ALEX'S ACTIONS

Occasionally, hard things seem impossible. As a parent, help your children walk through what they need to be successful so they can see the difference between insurmountable problems and challenges they can conquer.

- Stay close to your child so you can know when it's appropriate to say, "I don't see what the problem is."

- Stay encouraging and positive. Telling your children that you know they can do hard things and reminding them they have all the tools necessary is far more effective than belittling them for feeling overwhelmed.

- Develop stamina through focus, determination, and follow-through.

- Remember: A "high" standard may look different from one child to the next.

Chapter 9

Power Tools for Parents

by Rich

Values are the bedrock of life.

I distinctly remember a tender discussion with my wife just after our third son was born. We discussed the great hope we had for our children, but our thoughts also turned to the crazy, upside-down world we lived in. So many bad things can happen! We then asked the question that many parents have asked throughout the ages: "How do we raise our children so that they will want to do what's good and right and grow up to be meaningful contributors to society?"

At this pivotal moment, we made the decision to become proactive parents and break the trends we saw around us. This was the beginning of some eccentric parenting methods that we borrowed, adapted, and sometimes even stole to apply to our family.

> We made the decision to become proactive parents and break the trends we saw around us.

Many individuals have asked about our parenting throughout the years, so in this chapter, I outline a few of the methods, tools, and practices that we have found to have significant impact on strengthening our family.

VALUES LIST

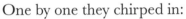

My noisy, little men fidgeted as their legs dangled off the couch, kicking in restlessness. My oldest, John, was eight, Matthew was six, and Nathan was three.

I stood in front of them and asked them a single question: "What is it that Christiansen boys do?"

One by one they chirped in:

"We're honest."

"We're hard-working."

"We're smart, and we're fun."

It was beautiful. Their mother's eyes welled up with tears. The lessons that she had been teaching them during their soft, tender years had begun to sink in. They went on to list other things—attributes, achievements, goals, sources of purpose—that they expected of themselves.

From the time each of my sons was very small, the Christiansen

> *The expectation was not set by Mom and Dad but by themselves.*

Boys list has hung above their beds, setting a benchmark—a compass, if you will—of what was expected of them. The expectation was not set by Mom and Dad but by themselves. The posters above their beds became very tattered. They were dearly cherished, and the boys have used them throughout their lives to help guide and direct them and launch them into adulthood.

Last year, I observed with great delight that my married son, who was just graduating from college, and my son serving others in Africa, still keep their Christiansen Boys poster on their walls.

Ask your kids what they stand for and what they expect from themselves. I think you might just be delighted to find out their answers. Then it is your job to reinforce those answers. Below is the list our boys came up with. Each family needs to create their own list.

CHRISTIANSEN BOYS

- Have an enduring marriage
- Work hard
- Learn to play the piano
- Are Eagle Scouts
- Dedicate two years of service to others
- Support each other
- Are nice
- Are smart
- Get straight As
- Have fun
- Are happy
- Are confident
- Have good friends
- Are responsible
- Follow Christ-like principles
- Serve others
- Are responsible leaders
- Are strong
- Are positive
- Are determined
- Are honest

MISSION STATEMENT

With fiery gusto, he marched back into the room he had left and held the mission statement in front of Nathan's nose.

Dr. Stephen R. Covey taught in his book *The 7 Habits of Highly Effective People* that a mission statement is not only powerful in a business setting, but it can also be used to great effect at home. His simple teachings sparked the initial idea for my wife and me to create our own family mission statement. Once our mission statement was created, we hung it on our wall, and several times a year we would refer to it in our family activity nights.

We did not realize how much impact the document was having until our children grew into their early teenage years. I distinctly recall one event involving my third son, Nathan, and his younger brother, Tim.

Tim is a funny, quirky boy who has always had eccentric ideas. Nathan, being a more pragmatic and structured individual, was heckling Tim one day regarding an informal club that Tim had set up in school called the "Froggy Club." After several biting comments and arguments from his older brother, Tim stomped out of the room indignantly.

At this point, I thought I was going to have to get involved.

As I started to get up, I saw Tim pulling the family mission statement from the wall. With fiery gusto, he marched back into the room he had left and held the mission statement in front of Nathan's nose. His finger pointed to a specific line on the mission statement that read, "Our family will support each other in our goals, ambitions, and honorable aspirations in life."

Tim then grunted in Nathan's face before he turned and stomped back to the wall, crookedly rehung the plaque, and marched out of the house, leaving his big brother speechless. I had to leave the room so as to not laugh. Point taken, Tim!

In hindsight, it is very clear now the great impact our mission statement has had on our family. Our children, now mostly grown, tell us frequently how important our family mission statement was in their lives. It helped them understand how they were to behave, what we as a family stood for, and the basic expectations our family had of one another.

We didn't preach from it, nor did we cram it down any of our children's throats. Of course, we talked about it and reviewed it several times a year—but the most important part was that it existed. It was simply part of the family.

A "mission statement" could sound rather contrived and trite. I encourage you to call it what you wish in order to suit your family. Regardless of what you call it, though, I strongly suggest that every family thoughtfully and carefully consider making one.

When you create your family mission statement, do it in a relaxed and hopeful manner. Go away for a weekend, and take that opportunity to write down what you stand for and believe in. Others may tease you—some values are certainly not common, nor is a family mission statement—and you may even get a bit of backlash. But don't let it stop you. I

Write what values you hold close to your heart.

promise that this is one of the most powerful things that you can do for your children to give them guidance, resolve, and context for the heart of your family. The ideas can even be passed on to the next generation. One of the first things my children have done with their wives after they married is create a family mission statement together and hang it on their own apartment walls.

Write what values you hold close to your heart. Your mission statement should be unique to your family. But if you need a guiding hand, here is the family mission statement my wife and I penned some 25 years ago.

CHRISTIANSEN FAMILY MISSION STATEMENT

Our ultimate family goal is to always love each other and be a strong family forever. Our family will support each other in our goals, ambitions, and honorable aspirations in life. Our home will be an environment of safety, love, and respect. We desire all who enter to feel loved and accepted. Our family will provide unconditional love for one another. We will always love each other, stick up for each other, and build each other. We will teach respect for people, places, and things.

We will embrace the value of hard work while teaching leadership and obedience to God's commandments. We will allow each other to make mistakes and grow from these mistakes, yet encourage one another to reach for higher levels. We will encourage each other to have positive friendships and relationships.

Our family will work together, play together, and stay together. We will laugh often, enjoy and savor the good, and fearlessly fight the bad. We will act on life and make the negative situations that occur in our lives become positives. We will value learning and education, foster development of self, and strive to reach a true level of self-actualization. Each family member will strive to make a meaningful, positive contribution to humanity in the chosen area of focus. We will always be a strong and loving family.

FAMILY HOME EVENINGS

Each week we have a family activity night, where we have a short discussion, play a family game, and then have a treat together. The discussion is usually held on Sunday night, while the activity is on Monday night. Sometimes we go bowling or to a movie, other times we see a play, and on other occasions we have a big family dinner.

The kids really look forward to it because it's a safe and fun time for us to all connect as a family. We don't overcomplicate things; we try to laugh, chill, and *not* let a bunch of interruptions happen.

Sunday afternoons and Monday nights are times we keep open in our schedule, and we do our best to avoid non-family events.

THE TRIP FOR 12-YEAR-OLDS

It was the third week of the trip, and I found myself nauseated, tired, and ready to go home. The mingled musty, rancid, and spicy scents coupled with the barrage of nonstop new sights overwhelmed my senses. One moment you would see children lying amid the garbage at the side of the street, and the next you'd see men, women, and children bathing openly in what appeared to be a sewage spill. Then you'd see motorcycles zipping everywhere, followed by an elephant or a camel. In that month, Nathan and I had seen much of India. We had covered a lot of land already, from the Taj Mahal to the slums of New Delhi. We had served in Mother Theresa's orphanages and met with business executives.

I have deliberately taken each of my children to a developing country on a father-and-son trip when they turned 12. It is something my sons have looked forward to. They have viewed it as their coming-of-age trip.

One moment you would see children lying amid the garbage at the side of the street, and the next you'd see men, women, and children bathing openly in what appeared to be a sewage spill.

It has helped them attain a global understanding of the needs of others and removed much of the selfish attitudes of entitlement that so many teenagers fall into.

The trip has served a very powerful purpose in enabling my children to see other parts of the world and more fully understand the difficult situations that most live in. It has helped them attain a global understanding of the needs of others and removed much of the selfish attitudes of entitlement that so many teenagers fall into.

During the trip, I have also been blessed with opportunities to have an open, trusting dialogue with my sons regarding what it means to be a man. After about the second week of exploring, eating, learning, growing, and hanging out together 24/7, my sons have been very open to conversations about how they want to live their lives. A special bond is created that can't be broken. These are the three concepts I teach them, which I consider to be the three primary duties of a man of honor: Provide, Protect, and Be Responsible.

One of the most powerful things you can do with your youth is to give them an awareness of the world around them.

Many individuals tell me that it is not possible for them to take a trip to India or Nepal with their children. I understand that this could be a huge financial sacrifice, but may I suggest Latin America? We've also taken trips to Guatemala and Peru, and even Mexico. Or, for some, maybe there is a local community you could visit. This can be done relatively cheaply. It takes a lot of planning, and it can seem a bit scary, but I'm here to tell you that one of the most powerful things you can do with your youth is to give them an awareness of the world around them. I challenge you to do it, and I promise you it will have an incredible impact on your teens as you raise them.

DOCTRINE, SYMBOLS, AND RITUALS

One night, before a unique opportunity to lecture at Harvard, I was invited to have dinner with a faculty member. Typically, the faculty member assigned to such dinners is from the business school; but, to my surprise, I had been assigned to dine with one of the faculty members over a religion department. I groaned a bit at the situation and had no context of what the discussion would be. As I arrived that night, my nervousness was quickly put to rest, as the professor was open, genuine, and truly inquisitive.

Our flag, the Statue of Liberty, the Liberty Bell—all are symbols that we look to.

The professor focused on the similarities between religion and government and the elements that are required to make both work. I was fascinated as he recounted the three distinct similarities that drive both religion and governments: rituals, symbols, and doctrine. Using the United States of America as an example, we have many symbols. Our flag, the Statue of Liberty, the Liberty Bell—all are symbols that we look to. We then have our doctrine, which is the Declaration of Independence, the Constitution, and our laws. We also have some interesting rituals. For example, when we recite the Pledge of Allegiance, we stand and put our hands over our hearts when the flag is presented. We also exercise our right to vote (and then accept the outcome of the majority, which we may find ourselves at odds with at times).

Religions, the professor noted, have these same elements. He then went on to explain that religions have the capacity to be much more fluid and have survived much better than rigid governments, because if any one of those three elements breaks in the government, often the government will fail. I was captivated by this concept. After three or four hours discussing the intricacies of

Our "Christiansen Boys" values list and our family mission statement are examples of family doctrine.

religions and governments, I asked him if he thought that these same concepts could be applied to families. He was delighted at the question, although he confessed he had not considered it. But he then replied, "Now that you mention it, of course. Look at the Rockefellers, look at the Kennedys, look at many of the great American families."

Although we hadn't thought in these terms at the time, I realized that Alice and I had aggressively enacted a legacy of rituals, symbols, and doctrine in our family. Our "Christiansen Boys" values list and our family mission statement are examples of family doctrine. Our family also makes use of symbols. Some years ago we even created a family symbol and logo.

The logo abstractly depicts our family. My wife (a gray circle) is in the center, with me (a black outline) surrounding, protecting, and supporting her. We are surrounded by symbols that represent our children, each an individual color.

Having symbols that your family can use as touchstones is very empowering for teenagers. Symbols help create a sense of identity at a time when many teenagers are trying to "find themselves."

Like symbols, rituals can be grounding within a family because they are shared experiences. The power is in the sharing, so it doesn't matter if they're a little silly. One of our rituals is to sing

Symbols help create a sense of identity at a time when many teenagers are trying to "find themselves."

a fun song called, "The Lord's Been Good to Me," from Disney's *Johnny Appleseed*. We always sing it from the balcony of our cabin the first night we spend there. We can't even think of being at the cabin now without my teenagers and grown children alike singing this song to the trees as the sun sets. The lyrics aren't particularly momentous or earth-shaking, but the experience of sharing the song together, in a ritual setting, is.

I promise you that forming rituals for your family can be a powerful tool.

More formal rituals also have their place. As each of my children comes of age, I present to him or her a ring with our family logo on it. I give one to my daughters-in-law when they enter the family too. When they receive these rings, they take on the Christiansen creed, which outlines how they are expected to live their lives.

Family traditions are also rituals: holiday traditions, summer traditions, vacation traditions. They bring your family together and allow everyone to bond with one another. These bonds help teenagers feel safe and happy and all the stronger for being part of a caring family.

I know that some people will view these as somewhat mechanical and contrived, but I promise you that forming rituals for your family can be a powerful tool. If you deliberately deploy them, just like religions and governments do, you will create a lasting, stronger, and more powerful family.

FAMILY DINNERS

It is important to provide opportunities for your family members to be open with one another and to spend time with each other. It is important

to provide a venue for this sort of communication on a regular basis—ritual-like, if you will—so it becomes natural. In addition to other family times I've already discussed, we have regular family dinners. A minimum of once a week, we have a formal setting in which everyone sits around the table, and each person highlights a positive and negative aspect about their current selves. Our family is happiest when we do this three or four times a week, not just once. If you're not taking the occasion to sit down as a family and have a delicious dinner together, start doing it.

COLLECT SOMETHING

One of our family's passions is climbing mountains. When our children were young, we started the tradition of bringing home a small stone selected by one of our children from the top of each mountain we climbed. Not giving the growing collection a lot of thought, I created a shoddy board and began supergluing these rocks onto it, listing the hike of origin below each one. Fast forward some 20 years, and we now have several boards chock full of rocks.

When my wife and I die, I'm not concerned about the children fighting over anything except the rock boards. You'd be surprised how many memories can be represented by small objects you collect as a family, each one a symbol of your experiences.

It honestly doesn't matter what you collect: butterflies, pins, Pokémon cards, Christmas bells, or horseshoes. Whatever your family passion happens to be, start a collection, and make it public. It will shock you how this turns into a symbol for your family and your posterity.

GOALS

There is already a chapter in this book that talks about personal goals, but I encourage everyone to make family goals, as well.

Our family sets goals twice a year: once in the summer and once on the first day of the New Year. Our goal-setting process involves everyone and helps each member of our family know what they're focusing on. It hones their thinking and helps them realize their dreams and aspirations. Setting goals together helps make sure everyone is operating on the same page and has a unifying effect.

Write down the goals, and post them on the wall. Your teenagers will be so much more encouraged if you write goals with them, know what their goals are, discuss them periodically, and support them as they pursue their individual goals.

If you're not setting goals, do it! It is not hard, so no excuses!

STRAIGHT-A DINNERS

One of the wonderful traditions handed down to me from my parents was the concept of a "straight-A dinner." The rule in our family has been that if you get straight As for the term, then Mom and Dad will take you out to dinner, and you get to choose where you go. If you get As, but some are A-minuses, you still go to dinner, but Mom and Dad choose the place. If there's even one B, then all bets are off. This tradition has proven to be a powerful motivator for our children, giving them the incentive, as well as the confidence, to do well in their schooling.

Now, I understand not everyone's primary focus is academics (our family deliberately made the choice that it would be when we first started having kids). I also know that this is a sensitive subject, and some parents may say, "My kid simply isn't built to be a straight-A student." If that's the case, that's okay; however, put some other mechanism in place that will allow you to teach them these principles. Rewire your children to think in these terms, and

> *My experience is that running and ruling a family with an iron fist seldom works.*

then quickly reward and encourage them when whatever goal you and your children set has been achieved. Goals with attached rewards are powerful motivators. My four brothers and I had very few terms during which we didn't get straight As, and there has been only one quarter in which one of my sons didn't get straight As. This method can help cut down the need for parental nagging. Give it a try, and expect to see some great results.

FAMILY VOTES

Give the entire family equal voice whenever possible (and reasonable). We do this by holding family votes. This helps all the children feel equally empowered—older sibling opinions don't count for more.

When there's a decision to be made, I present three or four options. I then require everyone to close their eyes and vote. The majority wins. Sometimes the poll is made on silly, inconsequential matters, such as which restaurant to go to, which hike to take, or which activity to do; but this is not always the case. Having your children weigh in on more consequential decisions allows them to be empowered and respected and tells them their voice matters.

My experience is that running and ruling a family with an iron fist seldom works. Teenagers respond well to decisions and accountability.

FAMILY VACATIONS

One of the things our family most looks forward to every year is our annual family vacation. We will typically plan it six to nine months in advance. We talk about options, we prepare, we study, we do everything we can to psych ourselves up for the vacation. It's almost as fun planning for the vacation as it is going on it. By looking forward to something and working on it together, you unite your family and bring everyone together. If your family isn't really a vacation family, you can plan for other things that are meaningful to you, like new furniture or a special local event.

> *Working together, playing together, dreaming together, talking together—it all sounds like a pretty good recipe for success to me.*

Your children should play an equal part in planning and preparing (age appropriately, of course). When our children were young, we set up a vacation jar, and my wife and I asked each of our sons to contribute to it. If there's some sacrifice on the part of the children, the vacation becomes more meaningful.

We have taken this idea to a further level as our children have gotten older. As I've described, our boys have been able to build a number of successful businesses, and one of the few things the profits are used for is paying for family vacations (along with paying for college and educational opportunities in developing countries). This acts as an incentive, allowing our family to work together on a business while looking forward to a fun family trip.

I'm not saying you have to build a business with your kids in order to plan a family vacation. But you should find a way to work with your children so they're able to contribute monetarily to the vacation. If you do, you're going to get a big bang multiplier effect! Working together, playing together, dreaming together, talking together—it all sounds like a pretty good recipe for success to me.

CHEATING AND CHORE JAR

As our three oldest children reached their teenage years, my wife and I had some concerns regarding the video games they played— namely them using cheat codes in order to beat any given game. Although cheat codes seem like a small thing, it wasn't something we wanted to encourage. We also observed that our children's friends would often create characters that were, to say the least, not role models in any sense of the word—and this encouraged our children to do the same.

My wife and I discussed this, and we came up with a fun solution. She simply put a big jar on the counter called the cheating and chore jar.

At our next family activity night, she introduced this jar to our family, announcing that whenever anyone decided to cheat, whether it was on a video game, a board game, or anything else, they had to contribute five dollars to the jar, which would be put towards our family vacation. Our definition of "cheating" also included creating less-than-savory characters that leaned toward (sometimes quite literally) the dark side. Another rule we added to the mix was that you had to contribute five dollars to the jar if you didn't do your chores on time.

Naturally, it became the family joke—never was it a point of resentment or contention within our family, and many pointed jokes were made at its expense. There certainly have been a few five-dollar bills added to this jar over the years. Still, presenting the fine in the form of a reward has an amazing impact on curbing negative behaviors. Mom and Dad have even been known to have to cough up five dollars now and again.

THE RECIPE FOR CRAZY BEHAVIOR

My younger brother has a dog named Otis. As a pup, Otis loved to chew. Every time you stepped into my brother's house, Otis would wrap his slobbery mouth around anything of yours he could find. Frankly, it drove me crazy.

One day, as I was sitting on my brother's couch, I decided that if Otis really wanted something to chew, I'd make sure I obliged

Right when we started thinking that we had messed up as parents, they had worked out their issues for themselves.

him. When the dog grabbed my hand, I didn't pull it back. Instead, I shoved it deep into his mouth, and I didn't have a mind to retrieve it.

Although Otis did not have the capacity to speak, his body language said: "You're crazy! What are you doing?" After that, Otis never put his slobbery mouth near me again.

One of the most challenging things we've faced as parents as our sons grew up has been during what my wife and I call their "crazy phase." This happened with each of our sons multiple times. At this phase in their lives, we tended to become gravely concerned about some weird, disconcerting quirk, negative behavior, or outlandish idea. However, right when we started thinking that we had messed up as parents, they had worked out their issues for themselves.

What I have discovered in recent years is when your kids go through their own "crazy phase," there are three ways to deal with it:

1. Fight them on it. My experience has been that this response makes them hang onto the behavior longer.
2. Use the Otis method and let them get a taste of their own behavior.
3. Ignore and don't reinforce the behavior.

Options two or three are usually the best for dealing with negative behavior. There are times when serious action needs to be taken, though, and option one is also correct.

It is common for many parents to directly address a problem when issues arise. These approaches frequently include withholding attention, finding an appropriate discipline to curb the behavior, and establishing boundaries.

Wouldn't a better solution be to inject more fresh water into the contaminated jug until the offending object is brought to the top and naturally exits the jug on its own?

Of course, there are times when teenagers require these strategies, but most of the time I think they cause rebellion. I have observed that when youth are acting out, they are frequently seeking attention. When this happens, I think these three steps should be followed.

Step one: try to look at the issue through your children's eyes, and seek to understand their perspectives.

Step two: Spend time with them, and show interest in the activities and hobbies they enjoy.

Step three: After you have reached a place of trust, you can point out, in a non-shaming, non-attacking way, their concerning behavior and the consequences of their actions.

Love always trumps everything else with teens.

In short, overflow the problem with love. Picture a big jug of water with a long, thin neck. Imagine that something falls into the jug to pollute the water. What do you do? How do you get the foreign object out of the jug? Most people immediately begin using some sort of tool, like a stick, to dig out the offending object, thus disturbing it and often causing the water to become more polluted. In desperation, they then try to dump the water out.

Wouldn't a better solution be to inject more fresh water into the contaminated jug until the offending object is brought to the top and naturally exits the jug on its own?

Teenagers—and, really, all of us—are like this. If we receive an abundance of unconditional love and acceptance, many of our little bad habits, negative behaviors, and "crazy phases" resolve themselves.

This is easier said than done, but love always trumps everything else with teens.

THE VITAL COMINGS AND GOINGS

Your children's comings and goings are critical! You need to give focused intervals of attention during these times. When your teens leave the house, you need to look them directly in the eye, give them your full, undivided attention, and tell them you love them. When they return, you need to do the exact same thing. No matter how tired you are, when your child comes in for the evening, get up, embrace them, and give them your full attention.

I've met a number of parents who think they need to sit around and watch their children at all times, which is something I believe is unnecessary. However, during their daily comings and goings, you should give them your undivided attention, even if it's only for a brief moment.

As a part of the vital comings and goings in our home, we say a prayer with our children as they leave each morning, and then we pray together again before they go to bed. This is a quick way to let them know you're present in their lives and thinking about them.

Give this technique a try. You'll be surprised at how much a short amount of real focus at the right time does for your relationship with your teenagers.

Chapter 10

Don't Become a Sith

by Tim

Make good choices.

The basement was dark, except for a single, ominous source of light. The only sound breaking the silence was the hum of a fan from an overused video game console. A moist draft that smelled of sweat and stale popcorn enveloped the large room.

"Bwahahaha!" An unknown sound shattered the near-silence.

Gavin, a 15-year-old boy, somewhat shaken from the noise, entered the room to find his friend Tony laughing viciously at the results of his video game.

"Why are you laughing like a mad man?" Gavin teased.

"I just used my invisibility ring to steal all of the pillows in the game! Now nobody but I can sleep comfortably at night!"

> *"I just used my invisibility ring to steal all of the pillows in the game! Now nobody but I can sleep comfortably at night!"*

With one quick glance at Tony's character, he pulled the console's plug.

Gavin rolled his eyes and snorted at his friend, "I was only in the bathroom for a minute!"

Tony gave a cruel smile as he called up the Star Wars game's statistics screen. As Gavin watched, he let out a yelp when he saw Tony's character. It was an over-muscled man with a shaved head, yellow eyes, and a pale face covered with scars. His face was locked into a permanent scowl, and he wore black and red robes. However, the most defining part of the character was the background that surrounded him: a deep red that transitioned into jet black, with blazing flames and flashes of red lightning surrounding him. The scene would have given any child a nightmare—Tony made his character a Sith Lord, a villain of the Star Wars universe.

Gavin could only muster an awed reply that matched his horrified face. "My dad wouldn't like that," he stuttered.

Just at that moment, Gavin's dad entered the room. With one quick glance at Tony's character, he pulled the console's plug. Silence loomed over them as the fan gave its final turn.

Tony broke the silence. "You could have let me save the game first! Or at least given us a warning." When Tony looked up, he could see that his protest had no effect, and he muttered a hollow "Sorry . . ."

Gavin took a moment to reflect as Tony muttered his pathetic apologies to Gavin's dad. The game Tony was playing was a light versus dark game. A player could control his character to do good,

Each time he accidentally made a bad choice, sending his character further to the dark side, he would instantly restart from the save point until he chose the best option.

to do good with a few mistakes, to dabble in evil, or to be truly awful. Tony had chosen the latter. Gavin contrasted that with how his father played the same game. Each time

"Tony . . . you are not a Sith."

he accidentally made a bad choice, sending his character further to the dark side, he would instantly restart from the save point until he chose the best option. His dad's character had developed into the exact opposite of Tony's, with an angel-like glow behind it.

The father put his hand up to demand the boys' attention. It took a moment to gather his thoughts, and then he began: "Tony, in life you can choose good or bad." He paused, waiting for Tony to digest that sentence. "It may seem funny to become an evil character in a video game; but, in reality, that can set you on a path to ruin someone else's life, and even your own." The father rubbed his hands: "Tony, you basically live here, so I am going to make you sign a contract, just like I would do with any of my children who need help with an issue. Every time you choose to do evil in a game at my house, you will owe me five dollars. If you obey the contract, then you can continue to play video games here."

Tony, not understanding, asked, "Why would it matter if I chose the dark side? It's just a video game."

"When you are young," the father replied, "there aren't big choices that make all of the difference. But as you continue to make small bad choices, they grow bigger and bigger until you embrace those big bad choices." Then he finished: "Tony . . . you are not a Sith. Please, don't become one."

ALEX'S ACTIONS

People try to make choosing the wrong direction seem amusing and enjoyable when, in reality, it is not. Help your children understand this by setting clear guidelines and teaching them to evaluate and make the best choices.

- Warn your children about peer pressure that could lead them into doing wrong just because it is popularly accepted. Encourage your children to stand up for what is right, even when others tell them it is wrong.

- As John Wayne said, "Life is tough, but it's tougher when you're stupid." Help children see how, in the long run, wise and correct decisions make life easier.

- Life always brings challenges. Encourage children to find positive outlets and methods for handling those challenges. Otherwise, these challenges can shove them off the right path and teach them to find their approval and acceptance in less than ideal places.

Chapter 11

Teaching Kids about Money

by Alice

Prepare your children for financial success.

When Rich and I were first starting out as a married couple, we knew we wanted our kids to be humble. Once we started to make a good sum of money, we decided we didn't want our kids to know about it. We felt that having them grow up in a hardworking, humble environment was the best way to teach them to work for the things they achieved, rather than having things just given to them.

We had both grown up in homes where we did not talk about money: it was a taboo subject, right up there with sex, drugs, and porn. I remember my father telling me, "You never ask a man how much money he makes." He would get defensive about the subject of money any time the issue

> *I remember my father telling me, "You never ask a man how much money he makes."*

> *Most of what I learned about money I learned because I knew our family didn't have enough.*

came up. Sure, we received advice like "don't go into debt" or "save for a rainy day." But most of what I learned about money I learned because I knew our family didn't have enough. Really, I had to figure out my own way of getting the things I wanted—which was made easier by a good education and hard work. So neither Rich nor I were prepared to be open with our children about money.

However, Rich and I had a huge mindset shift after talking to a friend who did grow up in a good family that had a lot of money. He explained how you would not expect your children to know how to drive a car without any instruction. Why in the world would you *not* teach your kids how to handle finances? Why in the world would you not discuss sex and pornography and money and all of the other taboo subjects with your kids. If you do not teach them, someone or something else will. Why not start early and ingrain in your children the proper way to handle finances.

He went on to tell us that his parents wanted him and his brothers to be prepared to handle their inheritance or any family business that might come their way. He asked: "Would you never talk about the family finances and then, when you are ready to give your kids an inheritance, just dump on them a large sum of money and never teach them how to handle it?"

If you have made a few financial mistakes, wouldn't it be so much better to let your kids know about it so they can learn and avoid those same mistakes. Yes, sometimes it is embarrassing to admit that we have made mistakes to our children, but there is so much to learn from these mistakes. This is when we shifted gears and decided to prepare our children to manage their own money so that no matter how much money they make or are in charge of, they have the ability to be wise and make good financial decisions. Learning to make and use money are skills that all kids will need for the rest of their lives.

Knowing that, we make sure that, around the dinner table, our family discusses all sorts of subjects, including money management and business. Since they were young, our children have heard about business models and discussed what makes a good business (and what doesn't). Through these discussions— and through other lessons about hard work and commitment—our sons gained foundations for solid financial habits.

> *Put your financial mistakes to good use and let your kids know about them.*

When Alex, our youngest, was about seven years old, he decided to try his hand at a business endeavor. Without consulting anyone else, he used his crayons and paper and started making flyers. He went around the neighborhood armed with plastic bags and a stick, carefully picking up any dog poop he saw on the neighbors' lawns. After he picked up the poop, he knocked on the door and handed each delighted neighbor a handmade flier that read: "Dog Poop Removal $5—First time is free."

In his most businesslike voice, he told them that he had picked up their poop this time and would happily return each week for the minimal price of 5 dollars. He would then look them in the eye and offer to shake their hand to seal the deal. The neighbors laughed and were delighted. Unfortunately, this cute little boy's

While you are running errands, bring your kids, and tell them what you are doing—even when they are little.

mother heard all about it and decided that her seven-year-old had a few too many things to do with his time—like schoolwork and piano lessons—to be tied down to spending hours going around the neighborhood picking up poop. But the seed of entrepreneurship had been planted.

Alex saw a need in the neighborhood, and he knew he had the talent and resources to solve the need. He had learned that hard work pays off and that he could increase his cash flow if he had a business.

It's easy to talk to your kids about your successes—Alex was inspired by *successful* businesses—but what about your mistakes? Admitting failure and acknowledging that you're human can be embarrassing. But there is so much our children can learn from these mistakes!

Put your financial mistakes to good use by letting your kids know about them. Then they can learn to avoid similar situations, or at least how to dig themselves out of financial holes. Wouldn't you prefer that your kids not make the same mistakes you did?

Lessons about money and finances don't have to come in the form of lectures and spreadsheets, but they should start when kids are young. While you are running errands, bring your kids, and tell them what you are doing—even when they are little. It will make the errands less boring for them, and they will grow up knowing why Mom and Dad go to the bank, to the post office, to collect rent, or to pay bills.

I'm sure people thought I was strange when my little kids were in their car seats and I told them, "Mommy has to go to the bank. We are putting money in the bank." Then, when I would use the drive-up window, the children would ask, "Why is that thing sucking up all of your money?" This gave me the chance to tell them that the bank was holding our money so we wouldn't lose it. Money conversations don't always have to be in-depth discussions, but answering their simple questions and talking about money will keep the dialog open throughout their lives. They will want to come to *you* to talk about finances.

As your children grow, the lessons you teach should grow with them. A few months ago, my 13-year-old had a "Job Shadow Day." He has job-shadowed both his mom and his dad his whole life, but I wanted him to learn something new and important. I had him do our month-end finances. He had to reconcile the business account and pay the bills. I had him look at the statements and tell me why we pay them off each month rather than letting balances due accrue interest.

We talked about frequent flyer rewards on our credit card, and he was excited to learn that was how we were able to take our last family vacation. I told him that no matter what kind of career he chooses, he will have to learn how to take care of his money. This was a big step up from explaining why the bank's suction tubes eat our money, but he is also a lot older now—and he had been prepared for this experience.

Our training has paid off so far. Just this past year, our oldest son finished college debt-free. He has been saving his entire life, so when he met his true love, he could buy a beautiful diamond ring to propose with. They have purchased their first home with a good down payment, they have a buffer built up for six months' worth of expenses, and he fully supports himself and his wife with good financial habits. He is only 25 years old, and I already know he will always be able to provide for his family

He is only 25 years old, and I already know he will always be able to provide for his family.

and stand on his own two feet financially because he uses the same models that have been ingrained in him since he was a child.

HOW WE TAUGHT FINANCIAL LESSONS

There are many different ways to teach kids about finances. Each family has to find methods and means that work for them, but those methods should all teach the same basic principles: how to save, how to budget, how to spend wisely, how to navigate current financial systems, and how to work for what one has. Here are some of the methods we used to teach those principles while raising our family.

The Jar System

When our kids were little, we gave them four jars to help them divide and budget their money wisely. We had to teach a few of our kids not to swallow the coins before they put the money in the jars, and we also encouraged them to decorate the jars. Each jar held a certain percentage of the kids' money for a specific purpose.

We had to teach a few of our kids not to swallow the coins before they put the money in the jars.

- **10% Charity/Tithing:** Setting aside money to help others allows our kids to learn to give back and to be charitable.

- **20% Long-term Savings:** Kids should learn to "pay themselves" to increase wealth. When our kids were little, if they earned larger amounts all at once, we increased this to 40 percent. This jar is where they saved for their own college tuition and religious or humanitarian services. It was from the savings account that grew out of this jar that our oldest son saved enough to put a down payment on a house immediately after graduating college.

- **30% Short-term Savings:** Not all savings should be for the distant future, or it is hard for young children to see the point in saving. Short-term savings are for more immediate things that they are working toward. Maybe they really want a new bike. They can save all spring long (or however long it takes) and have enough money to buy that bike themselves.

- **40% Spending Money:** The final jar is where they put their immediate spending money—popcorn and movie money, day-to-day money, etc.

No Allowance

The jar money did not come from allowances—we do not believe in them. Our kids need to learn to work, and they do not get paid for taking up space in our house or for doing basic household chores like making their beds and helping with the dishes. But we do provide ways for them to earn money. In the summer months, we pay them to mow the lawn. In addition, we teach them how we want the lawn mowed and then pay them according to the outcome. Tasks could also include extra-mile projects such as scrubbing baseboards, cleaning the cabinets, etc. We have rental properties, which require a lot of work, so we will "hire" our boys to rip up carpet, fix plumbing, paint walls, lay sod, build sprinkler systems, and do many other jobs. These tasks are invaluable. Not only do our boys earn income, but they also learn valuable skills that will help them throughout their lives.

The jar money did not come from allowances—we do not believe in them

Early Bank Accounts

As our boys got older, their jars became bank accounts. Hopefully, your bank has a patient teller, because sometimes it takes a while with kids. But we have found that having our boys do their own banking is invaluable. It is scary for them the first time they have to go to the bank teller and cash a check or deposit money, but it helps them to start good habits.

To start out, we had them take their jars of money to the bank and taught them how to open an account. They had several accounts, just like their jars. Their checking (or debit card) account is where they put their spending money; their long-term savings went into another account, hopefully one that made a bit more interest; and short-term savings were put into another account (or sub-account of their main account). To create a habit of charity, there was no account for their 10 percent to help others. They paid their 10 percent each time they got paid.

It is fun to see that my teenage boys still have their jars—but once the jars are full enough, off to the bank they go.

Debit and Credit Cards

As soon as they are old enough (policies may vary from bank to bank and state to state), help your children get a debit card and, later, a credit card. Some parents are wary of giving their kids plastic, but I would rather they make a mistake with a low-balance debit card than think they can charge huge amounts on credit and pay for that mistake for years. A debit card helps them learn to spend only as much as they can afford, which creates good habits before using credit.

Once they have a credit card, teach them how to use it. Teach them to read the statements and to pay off balances every month to avoid paying interest. Credit can work for you, or you can work for credit. Most banks have some kind of youth program with a low credit limit. These are perfect tools to use in teaching your kids how to manage money under your watch.

We also teach our kids how to use and get the benefits of credit card reward programs. We have used our reward points to be able to travel together as a family and have family experiences. It is fun to watch our grown children maximize rewards for their activities.

Freedom to Spend

We learned that we needed to allow our boys to spend money from time to time. It's easy to micromanage our kids and tell them what they can and cannot spend money on, but experience is a much better teacher than a lecture. Once they spend their own hard-earned money on something stupid, they realize their mistake much more quickly and avoid similar situations in the future. I would much rather have my kids waste 20 dollars as a kid and feel bad about it than have them lose 100,000 dollars or more as an adult and be blindsided—or, worse, ruined financially.

Responsibility for Mistakes

When our son Matthew was about 12 years old, he was learning how to play golf. He decided to practice on the front lawn. Unfortunately, he had learned to hit the ball farther than our yard extended, and he whacked the ball right into the rearview mirror of our neighbors' car, shattering it completely. Because it was his mistake, Matthew had to come up with the money to pay for the repairs. He came up with the idea to find lost golf balls near a local golf course and sell them to the golfers. It took him several weeks to make enough money to pay the 75 dollars it cost to fix the broken mirror, but the lesson stuck. He is responsible for his mistakes, and he has learned he needs to be able to pay for them.

Family Vacation Funding

Traveling as a family is something our family really enjoys. But Mom and Dad do not pay for family vacations. To fund our trips, we create some kind of a family business or opportunity that has all of us saving for the vacation together. This gives the kids more ownership of the vacation, and they enjoy it more because they had to help pay for it.

CONCLUDING THOUGHTS

When it comes to money (as with most things), kids need some help developing a philosophy, settling on an approach, and developing habits. Rich and I have our priorities and patterns, which we've passed on to our children through discussions, tutorials, and frequent reminders.

Your priorities and approaches likely will differ some, which is as it should be. But do take an active approach with your children, especially at a young age. Leaving money management to chance likely won't lead to the results that will be in their best interests—or yours!

ALEX'S ACTIONS

I can usually think of lots of things I'd rather do than talk to my parents about money. And I can *definitely* think of lots of things I'd rather do than work to raise money for my education, for vacations, and for other things I plan to do when I'm older.

I'll also admit that sometimes I've felt my parents' approach isn't fair, because I have friends whose parents pay for anything they're doing.

But, even though I'm still young, I've learned that it feels good to make a financial plan and stick with it, to come up with ideas for making money, and to contribute to the things our family does.

- If you haven't talked to your kids about money, do it!
- Remember: Forming and following through on a financial plan is emotionally satisfying.

Chapter 12

Building Businesses with Your Kids

by Rich

Give your child business experiences early on.

One of the most powerful gifts we can give our children is to teach them how to be financially independent. I'm not talking about leaving our children a big inheritance or instructing them on how to apply for jobs; I'm talking about teaching our children how to become rainmakers, how to weave straw into gold, and how to thrive in a turbulent global economy.

I think we all agree that there is no such thing as "job security." It is no longer the norm to get a job and expect to work there for the rest of your life. Formal, traditional education is no longer a guarantee that you are going to have a stable financial life. The ultimate security is teaching your children how to

> *The ultimate security is teaching your children how to create their own businesses and thrive in life, irrespective of what the economy is doing.*

create their own businesses and thrive in life, irrespective of what the economy is doing.

As I've traveled and lectured on business topics, the question I am most often asked is how I teach my kids to build businesses. In this chapter, I will share with you what our family has done. I don't claim that we've figured everything out, and our system might not be the right system for everyone, but we have done some interesting things that have been a lot of fun.

There are many facets to developing businesses with your children. First, you need to help them develop a mindset that will help them come up with ideas. Second, you need to create a culture of entrepreneurship and independence within your family. Third, you and your children need to understand how to actually build a business. Fourth, you need to ground your endeavors in ethical, educationally helpful ways.

THE MINDSET OF SEEING

There are three specific things we should teach teenagers to do to get them in the right mindset to create businesses: look for problems, consider how to solve them, and find ways to contribute.

Look for Problems

Always be on the lookout for problems, deficiencies, inefficiencies, challenges, or difficulties that you encounter day to day (even little ones). If you practice identifying these problems often enough with your kids, they should be able to stand in a room, no matter the situation, and identify problems. Most people are completely oblivious to these problems and block them out, almost like a storm door blocks out the wind and helps you happily ignore the fact that there is a storm howling outside. Instead, open the door and begin looking for the little issues or problems that surround you.

Consider How to Solve Problems

After you and your children identify problems, ask how those problems can be solved. This can be a very fun exercise—for both you and your children—as you become accustomed to scouting for problems. You may be surprised when your children start up conversations in the car at a fast food drive-thru about its inefficiencies and then come up with ideas that would allow the restaurant to move more cars through the system and make more money.

Identifying solutions is generally not rocket science, and the actual solutions don't need to be complicated. They can be as simple as you want them to be. Sometimes all it takes is asking how a problem could potentially be solved.

Find Ways to Contribute

Solution-finding helps take problem-finding from a destructive space (always seeing the negative) to a productive one. One simple question—"What can I do to contribute?"—is a powerful mindset to instill into your children. It helps them learn how to become successful entrepreneurs *and* community members. The opportunity to encourage your children to be part of solutions in society is one that justifies building businesses with them, regardless of any financial benefits.

CREATE A CULTURE OF ENTREPRENEURSHIP AND INDEPENDENCE

Benefits aside, building a business can be a large hurdle to leap over if it isn't something you or your children ever think about. It is important to foster a culture of independence in your home and present entrepreneurship as a path to that independence. This will keep both opportunities and solutions in the minds of both parents and children. It is also important to establish appropriate expectations for parent-child businesses and to treasure different types of success.

Create a Culture

In our home, we create an environment that helps build a need for independence. We make it clear to our children from a young age that we will not pay for their college tuition, their personal expenses, their vacations, or any other major activities. That being said, we *will* help them build a business so they can pay for these things themselves. Businesses have become a metaphor for life in our family, and they have helped us raise and teach our children to be responsible, productive, and independent.

> *We make it clear to our children from a young age that we will not pay for their college tuition, their personal expenses, their vacations, or any other major activities.*

Admittedly, we're not a typical family. When many families get together, they prefer to talk about the football game, current events, or the latest movies. It might sound strange, but my family frequently sits down and has a conversation about a business idea or a new business concept. This isn't for everyone, but it works for us.

Over the years, we have created a number of very successful companies with my boys. My second son, Matthew, was the first child to begin a family business. He was always very involved in technology and computers, and when he saw what I was doing with my advertising model, he asked if he could build one. We created a simple website about travel, and before we knew it, he was making 100 dollars a day as a seven-year-old.

> *We created a simple website about travel, and before we knew it, he was making 100 dollars a day as a seven-year-old.*

Needless to say, his older brother soon decided he wanted in on the website building too. Since then, coming up with business ideas and acting on them has become a central part of our family's interactions.

Set Expectations

Businesses are much more than ideas and hard work, and they rely on many factors to succeed. Even for the best business people, some ideas pan out, and some don't. Likewise, some of our fledgling businesses have worked, and some haven't; however, the not-as-financially-successful businesses (some of which were outright failures) were some of the most valuable ones, as they still taught my children important lessons and skills.

Teach your children to view the businesses you build as learning experiences. They—and you—will profit from each and every experience, even if that profit can't be expressed in dollars. Setting personal education as an expectation for the businesses helps keep children focused on lasting lessons rather than fleeting finances.

Treasure All Success

With learning as the focus of your experiences, you'll have no trouble appreciating all different types of success: financial, personal, educational, and more. One of our most valuable business experiences—a website called 2tieatie.com—was a financial flop!

The site started one day when our family was discussing what people search for on the Internet. The top three most popular "how-to" search terms were inappropriate for youth, but the fourth—"how to tie a tie"—really caught our attention and didn't have much competition.

Over the next six months, the boys learned how to tie 20 different knots and used their money to contract out all the pieces necessary to build *2tieatie.com*. They contracted out the writing to a writer on the East Coast, scheduled videos to be filmed, ordered diagrams from creators in Pakistan, and outsourced the engineering of the website to India. Soon they were working with people around the world and learning to manage a global team and business. Within a year they had over 5,000

> *Soon they were working with people around the world and learning to manage a global team and business.*

unique visitors coming to the website each day, and the site was ranked number two on Google in the search results for "how to tie a tie."

At the end of the day, however, the website was a financial flop. People weren't buying ties when they were on 2tieatie.com—those visiting it already had a tie and were desperately trying to wrangle it into submission! So neither selling ties ourselves nor advertising tie sales for other businesses earned much money. We all learned together, even though the site never monetized well. The traffic, exposure, and skills the boys developed building this website benefited future efforts that *were* lucrative.

Over the years, we have built a number of businesses that didn't work, and several more that became highly successful. One of our successes came after the economy went through a major downturn. One of my boys suggested that we build a series of coupon-related websites. My two middle sons managed that business, which included 14 teenage employees they had helping them manage over 100 different websites in specific coupon genres. They had built a business that generated approximately 650,000 dollars of revenue annually and ran at a net profit margin over 40 percent.

As you build your businesses, I strongly urge you to consider, highlight, and treasure all types of benefits—scholarships, education, *and* finances—when defining success.

BASICS FOR BUILDING A BUSINESS

Once you have the right mindset, culture, and expectations, it's time to build a business. If you haven't gone through the process yourself, be sure to educate yourself before diving in with your kids. There are many ways to do this, but I would point you toward my previously published books, *Bootstrap Business* and *The Zig-Zag Principle*, as a place to start. *The Zig-Zag Principle,* in particular, goes over the steps and methods of building a business. This chapter can only provide a condensed set of business principles, but I think it's relevant to summarize a few of the ideas found in my second book. Specifically, there are three sequential "zigs" that we look to when building a business: driving to profitability, adding resources, and adding a scale element.

Drive to Profitability

The drive to profitability "zig" is when you clearly define how much time should be spent on the business (including its expected duration) and when you set monthly financial landmarks. The plan should also include how much money you're willing to spend and invest in a given business. My philosophy is to clearly define the point that brings you to profitability and then, with guardrails, run at it as hard as you possibly can. I never expect to fail; but if I do fail, I desire to fail efficiently.

Add Resources

Once you arrive at your financial targets within your decided time frame, your next "zig" is when you begin to add resources and more complex processes. In simpler terms, this is when you start hiring others to help you and create systems and processes for your company to abide by. This "zig" also has a financial target, a time frame, and resource constraints.

Add a Scale Element

A scale element is an element in a business that allows it to grow and flourish somewhat independently, not requiring tedious day-to-day processes where you trade your own work hours for money. A critical part of the equation is setting up guardrails. Guardrails are the guidance points that you refuse to violate. That is, how much time you'll spend at a maximum, the duration of your involvement, and what your company won't interfere with—each of which will ensure that you keep yourself, your spouse, and your children in balance and progressing properly.

ETHICAL & PERSONAL CONSIDERATIONS

Although the zigs tend to focus on deadlines and monetary metrics, never allow yourself or your children to turn the focus of the company exclusively to money. The last thing you want to do is create an entitled teenager and corrupt his or her values. Core values and appropriate learning for your child are far more important than dollars and cents.

Discourage Entitled Thinking

Money should never be the primary focus of these companies for kids. Their true purpose is helping your children develop skills, knowledge, and experience. Ironically, the world's focus on financial gain is what makes me most nervous about building businesses with my kids. But money, just like any other single interest or enterprise, should not be the sole purpose of your children's lives.

So far, my children have handled our forays into business really well, but we have certainly run into awkward situations. One time, in particular, my sons created a business and hired many capable employees—mostly teenagers like themselves. One day, one teenage employee pulled me aside and asked to discuss his compensation.

*The money was not as important as keeping ourselves
and our businesses true to our principles.*

I was shocked, because this young man had not worked at this company for any length of time that would warrant being considered for a raise. He was also being paid extremely well for a teenager with little experience. The company had bought him an iPad and a computer, and his job included his own office and desk. His last job had been at a fast food restaurant. During our conversation, he claimed that a person with his particular skill set should be paid 100 dollars per hour, and he insisted that his wage be raised accordingly.

As you might imagine, this didn't go over very well with me.

As my sons and I realized that this money-driven attitude was becoming pervasive in that company, we shut the business down, knowing we were turning our backs on a profitable business. But, in this case, the money was not as important as keeping ourselves and our businesses true to our principles.

Mold the Businesses to Your Child

This book is one of the primary businesses that I am doing with Tim and Alex. Sure, we will make money; but this initiative has also afforded us countless hours of planning, collaborating, and incredible discussions. This also happens to cultivate Tim's love of words and writing and Alex's methodical nature and skill with organization.

In addition to not overemphasizing money, I also encourage parents to make sure business opportunities are age-appropriate and to set the purpose and goals within the capabilities of an inexperienced youth. Your children have their own skill sets, so make use of them. An age-appropriate business should require children to stretch their muscles, but it should never be impossible. As my sons have matured, they have gone from building simple

Early in our marriage, we talked of our desire to raise scholars, not athletes; and I would gladly assert that raising scholars mixed with entrepreneurs is a powerful combination.

---

service-based businesses to developing and selling products online. For them, that progression has been a good fit. However, there are endless possibilities.

The key is to make sure the idea is molded to your child and to restructure it as necessary. Remember that your child is still a child. Remain flexible and willing to change, and grow along with your children. Also, never tie kids down to the business so aggressively that they lose all other opportunities in life.

Encourage Well-Roundedness

"Be nice to nerds. Chances are you'll end up working for one."

Youth is a time to acquire the benefits from as many experiences as possible. I get quite concerned when I hear some of my entrepreneur colleagues talk about how needless a higher education is. If their son or daughter becomes an entrepreneur, they say, then why does school matter? They speak of their plans to never invest in or encourage their child to pursue a higher education—even going out of their way to bluntly discourage it.

My wife and I personally believe this to be a big mistake. Early in our marriage, we talked of our desire to raise scholars, not athletes; and I would gladly assert that raising scholars mixed with entrepreneurs is a powerful combination. I love the statement that Bill Gates made to a high school commencement: "Be nice to nerds. Chances are you'll end up working for one."

Formal education provides many values and benefits that freewheeling entrepreneurship doesn't (for example, social development, a general knowledge base, and learning how to learn). On the flip side, our formal education system fails to teach some key financial management skills. Formal education and practical experience complement each other, and combining the two is a far better solution than ignoring either one. Likewise, multiple interests—music, team and solo sports, engineering, and more—can complement each other and create more interesting, capable, and empowered adults. No one thing, even a financially profitable business that encourages independence, should eclipse other pursuits.

Set up Safeguards

To keep business and money from overshadowing other aspects of life, it's important that you build in guardrails and boundaries as you create a business with your kids. This isn't so different from the way you would erect boundaries around their TV watching, video game playing, or socializing with friends. Guidance and guardrails are an essential part of parenting.

As our family started having our first big business successes, we recognized the need to create and enforce these boundaries. My wife and I took our children through the formal process of organizing a company and created an operating agreement and bylaws. We began by calling a formal board meeting, where I boldly stated to them that this company was theirs to run (they owned most of it)—but if they went out of bounds and began misusing the business, the business was set up so I was the final judge, jury, and executioner. As a family, we did our best to guard against entitlement and any other forms of inappropriate behavior (such as being dishonest, unkind, or unfair).

They know this money isn't going to buy them fancy cars and extravagant lifestyles, and they have made use of it in ways that would make any parent proud.

> *I know that building a business with your children can be done and that it can be an incredible, powerful tool for you to create good things with your children.*

We also kept our focus on these objectives: To pay for their education and personal needs; to pay for family vacations and activities; to create scholarships for the education of children in developing countries.

Our company, CCD (Christiansen Custom Dreams), has been very successful in these endeavors. We've enjoyed many spectacular vacations, from climbing the Himalayas to spending a month in Peru hiking up to Machu Picchu to traveling down the Amazon. We have also been very active in sponsoring service trips to developing countries, where we have helped fund many children's educations.

These guiding principles have been a source of comfort to me, and I am very proud that my sons have lived by them. They know this money isn't going to buy them fancy cars and extravagant lifestyles, and they have made use of it in ways that would make any parent proud. Your family's guiding principles and core values may be different from ours, but you should identify them, make them clear to your children, and use them to guide the way they make and use money. Please be careful not to misalign your kids' values.

This may all seem very challenging, but I know that building a business with your children can be done and that it can be an incredible, powerful tool for you to create good things with your children. Enjoy the experience. It's one of the greatest things we've participated in as a family.

Chapter 13

Who's Got Your Back?

b y   T i m

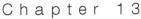

Kindness matters.

I know what it is like to be at the top of the peak and at the very bottom of a mountain.

I've always had the most amazing friends in the world, and I often consider them family. For as long as I can remember, I've had a blast with my friends. We've done everything from being pirates of the sandbox to peeing in my dad's office window well to being the goofiest kids in the school. I've seen many friends come and go, but only a select few have always been by my side to defend me. It's impossible to express my gratitude for such good friends. You can have as many friends as you want on social media, but how many of them would take a punch for you? What about a bullet?

> *We've done everything from being pirates of the sandbox to peeing in my dad's office window well to being the goofiest kids in the school.*

We would argue, fight, and forgive each other—but our friendship hadn't truly been forged.

Ever since we were little, my neighbor and friend Easton would come to my house, and we would see what mischief we could cause that day. We would stomp on broken light bulbs, dig large pits in the yard looking for "buried treasure," and clean out the whole fridge when we got hungry. At that point, Easton was just someone I hung out with for fun. We would argue, fight, and forgive each other—but our friendship hadn't truly been forged.

I remember the day I knew Easton was a true friend. I had just entered the first grade, and Easton was in the second grade. Not long after I started the school year, I became aware of a big bully the other kids called "Buzz." Buzz looked like a rhino with a shark's head and gorilla arms. It probably wasn't very kind, but many of us believed that Buzz would become a mass murderer after he got out of elementary school. He was so big and bulky, he even intimidated the teachers.

I don't remember how, but one day I came face to face with him alone in the halls. At this moment, he eagerly grabbed my scrawny arm and rolled up my sleeve preparing to give me what's known as a "rug burn." Just at this moment, Easton exited the bathroom to see Buzz start to apply pressure to my arm.

Easton threw himself at Buzz like a bullet, while yelling, "Buzz off, Buzz! Buzz off!" After this experience, Buzz never targeted me again, and I knew for sure that Easton was a true friend.

Years later, as I grew more confident and strong, I had one of the best years a student in junior high could ever have. I was trying out new activities, meeting

Buzz looked like a rhino with a shark's head and gorilla arms.

new people, and just having fun. I look back at that year and smile because I was fully myself. At one point, I even stood in front of my whole school in a dorky superhero suit and played the violin. When people started laughing at me, I just laughed along. I was the guy who stood up to the bullies. I was the guy who helped someone in the halls. The younger students looked up to me, and some became my closest friends. That year was my favorite because I felt like I was actually doing a good job as a junior high student. Easton was also doing well in high school. He was even dating around and discovering talents he never knew he had.

When I finally entered high school, I was excited to be in Easton's school again and share some more adventures with him. Sadly, though, once a short time passed, I soon realized that this wasn't going to happen.

When I first entered my foods and nutrition class, I was greeted by a new kid who everyone called "Cinnabon." Approaching me near the door, he said, "You won't last a week, squashmore!" Cinnabon then wrapped his hand in a fist and jabbed me hard in the ribs. I had no clue what to think. I had come into high school with high hopes for fun, but my first experience was anything but that! It continued for a week, and not much changed. Where was Easton? Where was my friend's support and encouragement? I'm not sure what had happened, but his support had just vanished.

The next semester I enrolled in a P.E. class and enjoyed participating in the various sports and activities. There was a problem, though. The older kids in the class would often lose to me. I guess they didn't like being beaten by a younger kid, because they would often spit at my face and call me nasty names. Once they even created a contest to see who could best surprise tackle me after I beat them in a simple game of ultimate frisbee. Worst of all, the coach made no effort to stop the behavior!

My smile got thinner and thinner, and the bullying got harsher and harsher. Through all of this, I didn't know what happened

All I cared about was surviving another day and finishing my math homework.

to Easton, and I quickly got to where I didn't care. All I cared about was surviving another day and finishing my math homework. I wondered why I couldn't be happy or have fun, and I only got sadder as the days dragged on. I told no one about the verbal and physical abuse I went through in that class, because I knew if I did, they would think I was a wimp.

I was truly alone. Some kids sat on the sidelines and just watched, and others joined in the bullying. There was no sympathy and no mercy. I was a walking punching bag for nine months. Then, just as I thought all was lost, something changed.

I discovered that a group of old friends actually still cared about me. Griff and Kade didn't know about the bullying or the pain I was going through. I never told them anything, but they could tell when I had a bad day, and they seemed to know when I needed an extra dose of kindness. Without even knowing it, they changed my whole life. It wasn't until everything was over that I told them about being bullied, but I knew that they would've fought for me, and I would fight for them. These friends made all of the difference in my life.

Each of us has the ability to either greatly build and help others, or to completely destroy them. We should all seek to be friends that build, support, and stand up for others. We should also actively seek out these kinds of friends for ourselves. With a few good friends, we don't ever have to be alone.

We should all seek to be friends that build, support, and stand up for others.

ALEX'S ACTIONS

Kids need to be nicer to each other! Seriously, no one should ever be bullied. But it happens all the time, whether it's getting beat up at recess or getting trashed on social media. Both really hurt!

And parents need to help kids be nicer—and to feel safe.

- Remember: Emotional bullying is harder to spot than physical.

- Keep your eyes open for signs of depression.

- Follow your children on social media. Let them know that you're not spying; you're just interested in their lives.

- Have open conversations daily that help your kids feel comfortable talking to and confiding in you when something big is going on in their lives.

Chapter 14

Getting Smart

by Tim

Teach your kids to work.

Todd was an eight-year-old boy living with his family in the small town of Dyersville. Although very capable, he wasn't the smartest in his class, nor the most athletic. But he sure knew how to work hard! As a young boy, he desperately wanted to earn money, so he started various small businesses.

His first business venture was selling night crawlers to old fishermen. This worked great as Todd would hunt for night crawlers during the night and then place them in a fridge in front of his home with a money box and sign advertising his product. Over time, Todd discovered that if he poured water onto the soil and then waited a few minutes, he could find the night crawlers quickly and easily. As Todd

With the help of his mother, Todd learned how to make candles and began selling them to artsy individuals.

systematized his little night crawler company, he found he could sell the worms without any heavy maintenance other than a few minutes each night.

This success gave Todd the bug and a newfound excitement for business. He soon began to seek other ways to make money, all the while maintaining his night crawler endeavor. With the help of his mother, Todd learned how to make candles and began selling them to artsy individuals. He continued with this and a few other business pursuits. Then, years later, Todd discovered that the most effective, but also strenuous, way to make money in the little town of Dyersville was through mowing lawns. Todd had gained a lot of experience by mowing his own lawn over many hot summers. He reasoned that while it was a brutal job, he could make the most money doing it.

After only a few weeks of mowing neighbors' lawns, Todd's rusty, old family lawnmower started to have problems. The young boy could only do one thing—learn how to fix it. He talked to his next-door neighbor who he often saw repairing tractors and read a few manuals at the local hardware store. With the help of a few neighbors and a lot of research, Todd turned his broken-down lawnmower into the best grass muncher on the street.

Eventually, the whole town of Dyersville came to realize that Todd was the best mower around, and he

After only a few weeks of mowing neighbors' lawns, Todd's rusty, old family lawnmower started to have problems.

moved from just mowing people's yards to taking care of the lawns surrounding many of the local businesses. Although Todd had a wide range of clients, there was still one job he wanted above all: to mow the lawn of the town's park. The difficulty Todd faced was that only the mayor's son seemed to get that job.

There was still one job he wanted above all: to mow the lawn of the town's park.

Although getting the job opening was unlikely, Todd was willing to negotiate and was convinced it was worth a shot. When Todd reached the town offices to meet with Mr. Holmes, the man who oversaw all of the town's grounds, he gulped. Mr. Holmes was a nasty, grumpy, old giant. His face was gruff, his manners were rough, and his forearm bore a tattoo of a naked woman. Every child in Dyersville feared this man, and most adults called him "Sir." It was as if he were a troll who stood between Todd and mowing the park lawn. Todd was sure that Mr. Holmes would give him the toughest job interview of his life.

After some discussion, Mr. Holmes and Todd agreed that Todd could have the job—that is, if he could impress Mr. Holmes with one mow. Frankly, Mr. Holmes was a man who could not be impressed even if his own son went to the moon, and this made Todd nervous. Normally, mowing nice straight cuts would be a breeze for Todd, but the obstacle in his way was the nasty hill going down the west side of the park. This was not the normal bunny hill, either; it was steep and full of all sorts of bumps and potholes.

Before Todd started mowing, he took a good look around. He remembered that the mayor's son tried to mow the lawn vertically, pushing himself and his mower straight up the hill, but Todd

Every child in Dyersville feared this man, and most adults called him "Sir."

115

Todd had cramps and sores all over his body, but he continued munching the steep hill away.

lacked the strength for such a physical feat. Instead, he decided to go horizontally after making a frame around the hill. That way, he could follow the grooves of the large mound.

Todd started pushing and shoving his lawn mower across the seemingly unconquerable park hill. It took him all morning to get the frame and would take him into dusk to blaze the nicely cut rows into the hill. Todd had cramps and sores all over his body, but he continued munching the steep hill away. It would have been easy to have rushed the job, leaving sloppy results, but Todd was not the type to rush perfection.

As Todd finished mowing the park lawn, he was shocked when Mr. Holmes approached him from the distance and said, "Good job! It looks better than it ever has before, and you've finished in half the time as the last kid! I expect you back next week." Todd gave a tired grin and thanked Mr. Holmes, who handed him his first payment.

Years later, Todd used the money he had saved and bought several more lawn mowers. He then hired and taught his friends to mow the lawns for him. When he had them trained to meet his exacting standards, he began spending his time repairing small engines for various clients. This led to Todd learning how to fix other things, such as computers and home electrical systems—and he began to make more and more money. Eventually, after finishing college and working and learning as much he could, Todd was running and managing large companies. Even then, his desire to learn

"Good job! It looks better than it ever has before, and you've finished in half the time as the last kid! I expect you back next week."

more and work harder didn't stop, as he sought to increase his intellectual and relationship capital with each new day.

This led to Todd learning how to fix other things, such as computers and home electrical systems— and he began to make more and more money.

These initial childhood experiences set Todd up for the rest of his life. It all started with some worms, candles, and a lawn mower; but Todd took advantage of the many opportunities he had to get smarter, to gain new skills, and to set himself apart from the normal, everyday person. He became empowered and successful. Just like Todd, we, as teenagers and adults, need to grow and develop our talents and skills and take an interest in the needs around us so that we may contribute to the world and reach our full potential.

We may not have a lot of money. But with a little guidance, some confidence and risk-taking, and a lot of hard work, we can change a can of worms and a rusty lawnmower into a great company that makes significant contributions to the world.

ALEX'S ACTIONS

In the animal kingdom, mothers tend to kick their infants out of the nest at a very young age (and fathers tend to vanish). But, as humans, parents sometimes want to keep doing things for their kids longer than they should.

I'm probably a lot like most teenagers, and I'm sure I could sit on the couch all day playing video games or checking out my friends on social media, while my mom and dad take care of everything that needs to be done. Fortunately, though, that's never been an option in our home.

I may complain sometimes, but I'm glad my parents are teaching me how to work, how to see work as an opportunity, and how to do a job well and take pride in it. I don't really know how a baby bird's brain works, but I'll bet some think their mother is being very unfair when they get pushed out of the nest all of a sudden, after mom has been providing all the worms they can eat for several weeks.

I've had some of those same feelings, but I also realize that my parents are helping me learn how to fly. So, don't let your kids off the hook too easily. We teens all need some pushing—and sometimes more than we're getting.

- Teach your children to work and how to take pride in a job well done.

- Don't be afraid to push your kids; sometimes they need the extra motivation.

Chapter 15

Blind Bullying

by Rich

Teach your kids how to deal with bullies.

Thump . . . thump . . . thump . . .

A basketball slammed incessantly against the wooden floor. Charles's 13-year-old, bright, vibrant blue eyes scanned the gymnasium's court. He dribbled the basketball down the court, determined to get it to its target.

Mark, a tall, muscular 14-year-old, growled at Charles. "Throw the ball to me!" he demanded.

Only two minutes and thirty-seven seconds were left in the game. Charles glanced at the score—37 to 41—and thought, "The other team is ahead, but we still have time to catch up if we're really smart."

Mark snapped again, "Throw the ball to me! Throw the ball to me!"

Mark was open, so Charles flung the ball to him. But Mark dribbled and lost control, giving the other team possession of the ball. The crowd groaned. Charles's team, the Hornets, responded with their very best defense, and his teammate Scott knocked the ball loose again. Charles recovered it and dribbled back down the court.

"Again!" Mark growled. "Throw the ball to me!"

Charles threw the ball back to Scott—Mark wasn't open. Scott quickly turned and scored. Only two points behind now. One minute and forty-seven seconds left to play. The other team dribbled down the court, coming fast, breaking. They shot! It missed, barely.

The ref yelled, "Hornets' ball!"

The team shouted, "One last chance to score!"

A teammate tossed the ball to Charles, and again he dribbled down the court, looking for the right teammate to pass to.

A flashback of a conversation rang through his head.

"My dad is coming to this game," Mark had told Charles privately, "and I want to score a lot. If you don't throw the ball to me every single time you get it, I'm going to beat the hell out of you."

Charles was athletic but not a fighter. "Mark, I'll throw the ball to you when you're open, but I can't throw to you every time."

Mark spat back, "Every time . . . every time. Or else I beat the hell out of you!"

The memory jarred Charles for a second, but he snapped back to reality. He knew Mark wasn't kidding—he was the town bully. He fought more often than most kids ate pizza, and he fought dirty and ugly. There was a twinge of fear as Charles came down, because he knew that if he didn't throw the ball to Mark, there

> *"If you don't throw the ball to me every single time you get it, I'm going to beat the hell out of you."*

would be trouble. Scott broke for the basket, wide open, and Charles threw the ball to him just as Mark called for the ball again.

Scott got the ball, shot it—and it bounced off the backboard.

"Aww," everyone moaned as the buzzer sounded. The Hornets lost 39 to 41.

The coach rallied his team together, led a cheer, and said, "It was a great game; we've only lost two this year."

Mark cast a glare at Charles and snarled. Everyone shook hands and headed out to the locker room to get back into their street clothes.

Afterward, David, Charles's younger brother and his constant shadow, walked with him through the darkened halls of the school. "You played a good game," David said. "You almost had them."

Charles unenthusiastically nodded. They proceeded down the school's front steps and past the old gymnasium, out toward the dark vacant lot connecting the school to the old vocation building.

Thump . . . thump . . . thump . . .

As the two brothers walked past some bushes, a shadow passed, and a cold, hard object smacked Charles in the head three times. Pain surged, and he felt blood oozing down the back of his skull. The object was not natural. What was it? It felt cold and hard pressing against the softness of the back of his skull. He collapsed, his feet falling out from underneath him as everything went dark. David, who had seen Mark jump out of the bushes holding a pop bottle, fled. The older boy was no match in a chase; David was far too wily and quick. He threw rocks at Mark before lunging at the bully.

Charles lay unconscious as Mark continued punishing him; however, David landed several blows to Mark's abdomen. The bully backed off, spewing a few curse words on his way.

> *Pain surged, and he felt blood oozing down the back of his skull.*

Upon Charles's return to school, he found his friends outraged—so outraged that they had felt it necessary to exact revenge.

Through much rousing and pressure, David revived Charles slightly. Then he carefully helped his brother get to the hospital, where Charles was quickly attended to. The beating was pretty bad, and Charles stayed home for several days—partly out of the pain and partly out of embarrassment.

Charles came from a soft, thoughtful, well-educated home. His father insisted through the ordeal, "Our family does not fight; we can talk our way through things. It is never appropriate to fight, and if this situation arises, you do not fight him back."

Upon Charles's return to school, he found his friends outraged—so outraged that they had felt it necessary to exact revenge. Charles was disgusted too. Where were the adults? Nothing had happened to Mark, despite the brazen beating.

That first day back, Charles's friend Donny said, "Charles, come with me after school."

Not knowing what was going on, Charles followed Donny out onto the football field, where 50 to 75 kids, including all of Charles's friends, had prepared a real "fair fight." There stood Mark, glaring at Charles with all the meanness he could muster, his scraggly hair flying wildly.

Charles had fought Mark and won when they were younger, but he didn't like to do it. Nevertheless, he was angry enough that he wanted to swing back. But one thought kept racing through his head—his father's voice saying, "Our family does not fight. I expect more from you than this." Caught in an impossible trap,

There stood Mark, glaring at Charles with all the meanness he could muster, his scraggly hair flying wildly.

Charles stood there, arms at this side; and despite the urgings from the crowd, he knew what the outcome would be.

Thump . . . thump . . . thump . . .

This time it wasn't the cold sound of a bottle against a skull, but fleshy knuckles against a soft face. Once again, Charles was not only beaten, he was humiliated in front of all of his friends. He fell to his knees, and Mark snapped, "You cowardly jerk."

Charles bowed his head. One of his friends escorted him off the field. He walked home, and it was not just his body that had been beaten but his soul, as well.

The next four years of Charles's life were miserable and lonely. The label of "coward" echoed deeply inside. His self-esteem was shattered, and he didn't know if his friends valued him or not. It was especially hard to know if his friends were distancing themselves from him or if he was doing it himself. Either way, he lost them all.

He spent most of his junior high and high school years coping with the loneliness. Although he was intelligent and talented, he felt scared and unvalued. He didn't receive any of the athletic or social opportunities he had enjoyed earlier in his life. Indeed, he defined himself as a coward and a loser.

With the encouragement of some adults and with a lot of hard work in school, Charles left the small community, went to college, made wonderful friends, and built an amazing life. Bit by bit, as his successes mounted, Charles realized that the high school labels were unfounded. He was a smart, funny, and charismatic leader. He was able to travel the world, have an amazing job, marry a beautiful woman, build an amazing family, and truly find happiness despite his difficult teenage years.

> *Bit by bit, as his successes mounted, Charles realized that the high school labels were unfounded.*

Some twenty years later, as he drove down the freeway, reminiscing about his childhood, he heard a familiar *thump . . . thump . . . thump.*

A flat tire. He pulled over and exited the freeway into the community where he had grown up. One of the individuals who approached him to help was Mark's cousin, Lance. "It looks like you have a tire problem, Charles."

As the tire was being repaired, Charles asked, "What's become of Mark?"

"Oh," Lance responded, "he's had a rough life. He's struggled with alcoholism, just like his dad. He has difficult relationships with his children, and his marriage is no picnic." Lance went on, explaining that Mark had no close friends and struggled with his life every day.

Once the tire was fixed, Charles paid, thanked Lance, and said goodbye. As he drove out of the town, he shed a few tears—some joyful, some sad. The difficult experiences he had endured as a teenager had ended up being a blessing. Charles had stood up for the underdog. He refused to give in to bullies. He had learned how to resolve problems verbally like an adult, not by beating up people. As difficult as his experience with Mark had been, he had learned how to stand alone and be strong, despite the feelings of rejection and loneliness.

Then a surge of compassion swept over him. "Mark, God bless you. I forgive you. I wish you well, and I hope that all will be well in your life too."

PACER'S NATIONAL BULLYING PREVENTION CENTER

General Statistics

More than one out of every five students (20.8 percent) reports being bullied (National Center for Educational Statistics, 2016).

64 percent of children who were bullied did not report it; only 36 percent reported the bullying. (Petrosina, Guckenburg, DeVoe, and Hanson, 2010).

More than half of bullying situations (57 percent) stop when a peer intervenes on behalf of the student being bullied (Hawkins, Pepler, and Craig, 2001).

School-based bullying prevention programs decrease bullying by up to 25 percent (McCallion and Feder, 2013).

The reasons for being bullied reported most often by students were looks (55 percent), body shape (37 percent), and race (16 percent). (Davis and Nixon, 2010).

Effects of Bullying

Students who experience bullying are at increased risk for poor school adjustment, sleep difficulties, anxiety, and depression (Center for Disease Control, 2015).

Students who engage in bullying behavior are at increased risk for academic problems, substance abuse, and violent behavior later in adolescence and adulthood (Center for Disease Control, 2015).

Students who are both targets of bullying and engage in bullying behavior are at greater risk for both mental health and behavior problems than students who only bully or are only bullied (Center for Disease Control, 2015).

Students who experience bullying are twice as likely as non-bullied peers to experience negative health effects such as headaches and stomachaches (Gini and Pozzoli, 2013).

ALEX'S ACTIONS

It is better to be kind, even when that kindness is not returned. Anger and violence beget anger and violence. Ask your children: Would you rather have a hundred friends or a hundred enemies? Would you rather the violence end with you, or would you rather perpetuate it and hurt others?

Explicitly discuss with your children how to deal with bullies. If they or people they know face bullying or harassment, they shouldn't be afraid to stand up for themselves or their friends. Teach them to be (1) clear and confident, (2) to try to resolve issues by talking through them, (3) to ask for help if they need it, and (4) to go to the adults in their lives. If one adult won't listen, find another who will!

Revenge and bitterness don't help anyone. One person's rudeness or cruelty does not justify someone else's choice to be rude or cruel. Teach your children to be responsible for their own choices in all situations.

Teach compassion and consideration. Children should be aware that sometimes what they believe is a fun joke can cause someone else grief, and the grief isn't worth the joke—no matter how funny they think it may be.

- Remember: It is better to be kind, even when that kindness is not returned.
- Discuss with your children how to deal with bullies. Teach them to be clear and confident, to try to resolve issues by talking through them, and to ask for help when they need it, especially from adults.
- Teach your children to be responsible for their own choices in all situations.
- Remember: Bullying is not a joke.

Chapter 16

Example by Trial

by Tim

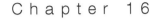

Walk in someone else's shoes.

"Josh is a jerk!" I thought while washing the dishes. My parents always sided with him just because he was three years older than me. He used me to do all of his chores, and he would get the glory!

Josh was off with his friends, enjoying the pleasant afternoon, while I stood over the sink, stuck in the kitchen, picking a crusted-on stain off his plate! I had to be his servant, and why? Because he was pulling off a 4.0 and receiving a bunch of "important" awards. It made no sense. Elementary school was easy; high school couldn't be that much harder. He was just getting lucky! I continued complaining to myself, irrational thoughts running wild, until Josh came home.

He threw the door open, and cool air brushed my burning brow. I set a fitful scowl on my face as I finished washing the table.

Josh tossed his backpack straight onto the couch pillow I had just fluffed. "Wow, Lane, this looks amazing!"

"Took me three hours," I said with a grizzly bear growl.

Surprised at my reaction, Josh looked up. "Is everything all right?"

I went back to scrubbing the table with twice as much fury.

Josh was shocked to see me act this way. I was the bright, positive brother, and it took a lot to bring me this low. Josh gently pulled the rag from my clenched fist. He spoke softly. "Lane, we need to talk, okay?"

"Fine," I grunted. He led me to the front porch under the stars.

Josh looked thoughtfully around before speaking. I just avoided eye contact.

"Lane," Josh said, "you may not be old enough to understand, but I was once in your same position."

"I doubt that, Josh," I scoffed. "Pete would never treat you like this!"

Josh spoke softly. "Probably even worse, if you want to know the truth. But that isn't the point." He paused long enough that I met his eyes, questioning. "The point is that I understand how you feel. I know it feels unfair, but when you're older, you'll understand what it's like to walk in my shoes. Life won't get any easier." He paused so I could register that. "I know we don't connect as well as we should, but we're still brothers, and we've got each other's back." He continued. "Lane, you are going to do great things. I love ya, Bro."

> "The point is that I understand how you feel. I know it feels unfair, but when you're older, you'll understand what it's like to walk in my shoes. Life won't get any easier. I know we don't connect as well as we should, but we're still brothers, and we've got each other's back."

At the time, the conversation meant almost nothing to me. But I calmed down and then almost forgot about it. But as Josh predicted, I did understand a few short years later.

Every day, I forced myself up a 5:00 a.m. for driver's ed, then sat through a series of honors-level classes, and stayed an extra hour afterward to get help with my schoolwork. Once home, I dragged myself over an unconquerable mountain of homework and finished around midnight. Then, after not enough sleep, the process repeated the next day. How had Josh managed the same exhausting load when he was my age? How had Pete done it before him? It had been three years since the pep talk he had given me, and now I had a pretty good idea what he was talking about. I wished he would come back from Mozambique, where he had been accomplishing miracles for the past two years.

It had been three years since the pep talk he'd given me, and now I had a pretty good idea what he was talking about.

After a particularly tiring day, I dragged my feet to the front door of my house. I only had one more day to get my grades up to a 4.0, and my driver's ed instructor had added another four pages to my mountain of homework.

As I came in, excited to finally eat something besides plastic school food, I greeted my younger brother by complimenting the amazing work he'd done on his chores. Then I watched as he got ready to throw a dirty pot into the dishwasher in anger. I gently took the pot out of his hand and asked, "Hey Bennett, will you come out to the porch with me?"

Today, when I look into the mirror, I see many of the traits that once frustrated me about Josh. But now I am proud of the similarities to the brother I love and admire. I often look at Josh's picture mounted on the wall and say to myself, "Thank you, Josh, for teaching me how to understand."

ALEX'S ACTIONS

Teach your children they are not the only people with emotions and feelings. Look for opportunities to help them understand what others are going through.

Life often seems unfair, but teaching your children compassion, empathy, and patience will help them cope with life's realities. Help them understand that not everyone needs the same things—be they benefits or challenges—at the same time.

Taking on a mentor or teacher's role helps us learn too. Sit down with your children and encourage them to think of one of their role models and make a list of the traits that make that person worth emulating. Then help them find ways to implement those traits in their own lives, possibly as a role model for a younger sibling or a peer who is struggling.

Just as Lane learned from Josh, and Josh taught Bennett, many people take things they learn early in life and pass those lessons on to others. Let your children know that your parenting is an attempt to help them learn lessons you've already had to learn the hard way. Encourage them to pay attention to what their own experiences teach them so they can teach well in the future.

- Remember: Teaching your children compassion, empathy, and patience will help them cope with life's realities.

- Encourage your children to emulate the traits of their role models.

- Let your children know that your parenting is an attempt to pass on lessons you've already had to learn the hard way.

- Allow your children the opportunity to work out their conflicts.

Chapter 17

"The Talk"

by Rich

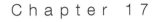

Talk about the hard things.

I remember very distinctly being a small, late-blooming 12-year-old and having my father take me to a church meeting where "the talk" was given. The talk was comprised of an elaborate metaphor about factories, gears, and not messing with the machine. There was nothing directly stated, and certainly none of the forbidden words were used. There were various analogies, innuendos, and delicate metaphors that, as a grown man, I am still not sure I fully understand. I had no clue what was being discussed other than it was a forbidden topic. Every man in the room, both young and old, had his eyes on the floor, and no one had any intent of ever revisiting this topic again.

That evening, my father handed me a pamphlet and said, "Well, as you start

> *Every man in the room, both young and old, had his eyes on the floor, and no one had any intent of ever revisiting this topic again.*

growing, things will start happening to you, and you will get more hair." That was it! The topic was never raised again. Needless to say, as I grew into puberty, I did not ask! This is an era where you simply didn't talk about sex with adults. Oh, there were plenty of kids talking about it, but in hindsight, most of what was shared came from confused friends trying to figure it out themselves.

My brothers and I now laugh ourselves to tears, as my younger, animated brother recounts the story of his "coming-of-age." To spare myself and also the readers from blushing, I will avoid the graphic details; but suffice it to say that when a 14-year-old young man experiences his first wet dream without any context or warning, a rather confusing set of emotions takes over:

- Delight
- Pleasure
- Shock
- Excitement
- Confusion

These are quickly followed by thoughts like, "Is something physically wrong with me?" and "What kind of a pervert am I?"

All of this is wrapped into a glorious, impossible set of raging hormones and emotions.

Once all of these emotions calm and settle, there is the dilemma of what you do next. My brother described the uncontrollable emotion of just wanting to crawl into a hole and never return.

My brother described the uncontrollable emotion of just wanting to crawl into a hole and never return.

You would think that we have come a long way in the past forty years, but I am not sure today's "maturation programs" are that much better. I have absolutely dreaded the mandatory school sex education presentations at my sons'

134

schools. At one I attended, the dads and their sons were awkwardly seated in a room with the door sealed tight. The teacher who had been assigned to this undoubtedly challenging task stood up and, in a very antiseptic manner, explained the mandatory bodily

He then showed a video of a cat getting stuck on a fan that was spinning around and around.

changes. He then showed a video of a cat getting stuck on a fan that was spinning around and around. The point of the video was something like, "The things that are going to happen to you are kind of awkward—just like this cat on the fan." At the very end of the presentation, the teacher mustered the courage to say words like "puberty" and "wet dreams," all while blushing. He then closed the discussion by saying, "We ran out of time," and rushed out of the room. As I discussed this with my sons, the only thing they seemed to remember was the confusing cat video. I am not sure this presentation was as bad as the talk I attended about factories and machines and not messing them up, but it was pretty close!

After five sons, I've been through this enough to know that we've got to talk about it. Talking about it is the first step, and there is honestly nothing to be ashamed about. My wife humorously tells the story of growing up on a dairy farm and then returning home to visit her parents some years later after being married and asking her parents why they never discussed or taught her anything about sex.

Her mom looked at her and replied, "Well, Sweetheart, there were the cows out there; that was your education."

My wife gasped in horror, saying, "The bellowing cows were who I was supposed to learn about all of this from?"

My wife also tells the story of a young woman in her P.E. class who began to scream and cry one day, thinking she was dying.

Nobody had ever told her about a period and what to expect. I am still appalled by how poorly most parents talk about sex and puberty with their children. My wife and I decided, as we got married, that we would talk openly, honestly, and very directly to our children about all of these sensitive topics.

As people ask for my advice, about my sons, how to create companies, and how to handle this situation or that one, I eventually see their eyes retract. And after skirting the issue, they eventually start to poke around and ask questions about the awkward, hard conversations they would prefer to avoid.

Their most common queries fall under the following three questions:

1. When do you start talking to your kids about the hard things?
2. How bold are you as you have these discussions?
3. What do I do if my child has become involved in a destructive habit?

There's nothing to be ashamed about here; however, our Victorian-based culture has our minds so tied up that we end up causing more problems than we solve when we actually *do* try to talk to our children.

Here, I will boldly promise you that by being transparent and talking openly and frankly to your children, leaving yourself open to calm and loving dialogue at any time and not allowing yourself to be bound by cultural restraints, you will create a deeper bond with your children. This honest transparency will encourage and allow your children to have more trust in you as a parent, and they will be even more likely to place their trust in you when it comes to the other topics that often entangle a teenager's life.

Children are never to be underestimated; your kids know when you are lying. They will know when you are skirting the issue. So if you have the courage to honestly talk with your kids on these difficult topics, then the other issues will actually come much easier.

> *Children are never to be underestimated; your kids know when you are lying.*

So when *should* you start talking to your kids about sex?

My wife and I began our instruction when each of our sons reached the age of eight. We took them to what has become a family tradition known as *"The Infamous Eight Date."* My wife brought out her nursing books, and we talked about sex. We reviewed the anatomy of both females and males, explained how babies are made, identified the reproductive organs, and covered what our son could expect—and when.

After this, our next parental conversation took place when our children were a little older (between ages 10 and 12). This is when I had a very candid talk about why abstinence is very important before marriage. In discussing abstinence, I also explained that sex is beautiful and good in a loving, committed relationship. I told them what they could expect when they experienced their first wet dream and then added that they shouldn't be embarrassed to come have a talk with me. Each of my sons has done this. These talks have actually created a wonderful bond of trust between us. I have never broken their trust, and that has helped them talk openly and directly with me about not only the sex questions but the other growing questions and challenges every teenager faces.

> *These talks have actually created a wonderful bond of trust between us.*

The key thing is to have enough open trust and confidence to have an ongoing dialogue. I will frequently check up on my sons and see how they're doing. With love, I explore whether they are struggling with pornography, inappropriate thoughts, or other concerns. Starting the dialogue when a child is young and having true trust moments have enabled the conversations to be ongoing between me and my sons, rather than a single awkward moment.

Shortly before our children get married and become sexually active with their spouses, we feel it is very important to have a detailed discussion with them about intimacy in marriage. No details are omitted in this conversation, and we do teach and cover birth control methods. As appropriate, my wife and I also sit with their future spouses and discuss any questions they might have. And, yes, they do ask very pointed and detailed questions!

I remember that one of the greatest blessings in my life came from my wonderful sister-in-law. As I was marrying my sweetheart, having grown up in a family of all boys and having been raised by parents who certainly had not had any kind of dialogue with me about sex, most of the things I had learned while growing up were full of awkward, teenage misunderstanding.

Several days before our marriage, my sister-in-law took me aside, sensing that I probably was a little clueless, and proceeded to tell me in very specific detail what I needed to know—and do—to please my wife. She used the analogy of a woman as a Crock-Pot slow cooker and man as a microwave. She shared with me not only techniques but timing, location, and other information. It has become a big, extended-family joke, but I sincerely say to her, thank you! I think she saved me five years of figuring it out.

Now before going any further, when we talk to my sons and my one adopted daughter about these things, it is a very private,

Starting the dialogue when a child is young and having true trust moments have enabled the conversations to be ongoing between me and my sons, rather than a single and awkward moment.

intimate discussion. And, frankly, talking to them face to face about sex is actually a little bit easier than talking about it on a printed page. But I want to share the mindset and teachings that we strive to instill in our children to establish a mindset of sex as something very special and that should be well guarded in their lives, as well as how to avoid and overcome the addictive traps of pornography.

SEX

We teach our children that sex is beautiful, wonderful, and exciting. It's the best thing that you could ever imagine. Anything you have ever heard about sex, it's actually better than that. But here's the key thing: it's a timing issue.

When a man and a woman begin getting really intimate with each other and they share this ultimate expression of love, it creates a deep, powerful, emotional bond. The purpose of sex, we explain, is to create a family and a bond that holds it together permanently.

If you use sex inappropriately and have these bonding experiences too young or too early, or when you're simply not prepared or mature enough to actually have children and form a family bond together, then sex ends up causing a lot more heartache and frustration and confusion than what God and nature intended.

It is true that, physically, sex feels really good—no matter what your age. But when the timing is inappropriate, sex is more of a lustful experience than a process of two people becoming closer together as husband and wife. When a couple engages in sex at the appropriate time, these special and intimate moments become the ultimate expression of love and pleasure between two committed individuals.

When a couple engages in sex at the appropriate time, these special and intimate moments become the ultimate expression of love and pleasure between two committed individuals.

> *It's not a matter of good or bad—it's a matter of timing.*

So, having the discipline to actually wait until you do get married—which creates a bond where you will have a meaningful one-on-one relationship and are fully committed to each other—will help you have far better sex. It will be far better because it is far more intimate and far more meaningful. The key is to wait until the right time. It's not a matter of good or bad—it's a matter of timing.

Waiting until marriage will create one of the most joyful, happy experiences in life, for both the man and the woman. Women can and do equally enjoy sex—and, in many ways, they can enjoy it even more so than men. Women are built to have more pleasure, but it just works a little bit differently and is very much a mental thing. You have to take more time, and you have to be in a real mode of trust; so, I challenge my young sons to control their sexuality so that when they do get married, their wives can trust them and enjoy sex as much as they do, if not more. Having someone you can fully trust and create a family with is the ultimate achievement of the human experience.

While I'm trying to teach my children these principles, the world whispers all these crazy notions that sex is just for fun—that we are nothing more than animals and should engage in sex indiscriminately. The world is sending our children the message that having sex is on about the same, uncommitted level as going to a movie with someone. What that ends up doing is dulling our senses, dulling our spirituality, and taking away the deep, beautiful value and meaning of these sexual acts. Even worse, such casualness deadens the joy that should accompany it.

> *The world whispers all these crazy notions that sex is just for fun, that we are nothing more than animals and should engage in sex indiscriminately.*

Men are wired biologically to be stimulated and attracted to women's bodies just by looking at them. I'm not suggesting we kill off our desires, but we do need to learn to understand and manage them. The reality is that happiness ultimately occurs by *being* committed. There's no greater joy in my life than the children my wife and I created together. Lasting happiness comes from living as a bonded, meaningful, and committed family unit, not from behaving like wild animals and not from "hooking up" with as many women as possible.

Of course, treating sex appropriately is no easy task. For some, it can be very difficult; but learning to control our desires is all part of a beautiful opportunity that awaits each of us. So the challenge I give you now is to learn these things yourself so you can better teach your children how to use this power properly. We should bridle our sex drive so it can guide our sexuality onto its intended path and course and reach our ultimate goal. Not only will the sex be better, but you will get more of it and at a higher level.

PORNOGRAPHY

With one click of a button, children and teenagers today can find any image imaginable. There is nothing that prevents them from doing so, other than self-mastery and self-control.

Pornography is a very challenging and delicate topic that most parents are simply ignoring. It requires leniency and understanding, yet direct controls. Some adults have the trite attitude of, "Oh, well; boys will be boys," and "he'll figure it out." This is a very dangerous mindset.

On the other hand, some parents think that pornography is so bad and terrible that if their children indulge in it, they are perverts and are destined for a life of nothing but trouble. This is also a toxic, counterproductive mindset.

Pornography is so prevalent in today's times and so broadly used that it is being called the new drug.

According to Mark Mauzy, Ph.D., men were hardwired to find the naked body extremely attractive. It's deep in our biology; however, think about how difficult it was for a man to see a woman naked hundreds of years ago. Typically, a man would only see his wife. I suppose if he were a king or nobility, he might have concubines and have easy access to a few other women——but the average man would only see one naked woman.

> *Pornography is so prevalent . . . it is being called the new drug.*

It wasn't until the birth of the printing press a few hundred years ago that people were actually able to create images meant to stimulate. But, even then, it was done very crudely. But now, thanks to the sudden and rapid advancements of technology, we became exposed to the world of full-color printing; and then, not long afterward, humanity was introduced to computers and the Internet.

It's only been during the last twenty or so years that people have had the ability to look at hundreds, if not thousands, of women or men in a matter of minutes if they so choose and indulge in the resulting biological hormonal reactions.

It's like combining crack cocaine, crystal meth, and heroine for sexuality! Is there any wonder pornography is so addictive?

So, how do we deal with this insidious vice?

First of all, I tell my sons that a woman's body is the most beautiful creation that has ever existed upon this earth. It was God's final and ultimate creation, and it should be celebrated and delighted in and enjoyed—within the bonds of marriage! However, the

> *It's like combining crack cocaine, crystal meth, and heroine for sexuality!*

problem with pornography is it messes up the true nature of intimacy. Those biological reactions you have for your spouse draw you emotionally together; but when using pornography, no bonding occurs. Instead, pornography creates a counterfeit form of intimacy, as it dulls the senses and warps the correct perception of what a relationship should

Instead, pornography creates a counterfeit form of intimacy, as it dulls the senses and warps the correct perception of what a relationship should be.

be. This is why the idea that pornography is good for society is the ultimate lie. It destroys families and weakens the beautiful bonds between a committed man and woman.

Are we naive enough to believe that our young men and young women are not going to encounter and maybe even struggle with looking at pornography at times? No matter what controls we try to implement and how diligent we are in policing our children, they are going to encounter pornography, either willingly or unwillingly. Given that, I personally believe the most important thing we can do as parents is to keep the dialogue open.

Power comes from hopeful, understanding, loving dialogues of transparency. The worst thing that can happen is for the issue to be buried and have it become a shameful, unspoken, hidden issue.

If your child accidentally stumbles upon pornography, he or she should feel comfortable talking to you, asking questions, or seeking your help. If your child is viewing pornography repeatedly, you should talk about it and help him or her look for positive substitutes that can effectively take its place. If your child has developed an addiction, there are counseling programs that can help rewire their thinking and emotions. But whatever the situation, a parent should never shame the teen that is struggling with pornography. This is one of our biggest challenges, because shaming a child guarantees he or she will never talk to you again about issues.

Some adults see the solution to the problem of pornography as banning cellphones, locking up computers, and not giving their children even limited access to technology. I don't think that this is a healthy thing, as it only creates children who, in the near future, won't be able to figure out how to make their own decisions and exercise the self-control they will need when they are on their own. Instead, we should teach our children to *choose* to be honorable men and women and to choose good, high paths. We want them to understand and later reap the rewards of having a beautiful, significant marriage. We want them to come to know that having a deep, meaningful relationship is far better than continuing down the path of lust and immediate gratification.

In our home, we help our children by putting various preventative guardrails and safety nets into place. One of the things we do as a family is put our cellphones (yes, the parents' cellphones, as well) on the table at the end of the day. Everyone in my family knows that we don't take our mobile-connected devices into private, dark places, including bedrooms. We have the computers out in the open and put filters on them to keep any inappropriate content from getting through (although no filter is perfect). We make it okay to talk about pornography—and if someone is struggling, I know and trust that they will tell me. When this occurs, don't shame them— hug them. The key is to talk openly and frankly and to create a safe environment in which your children feel secure enough to do so. Do not ever betray your children's trust.

The most important thing to remember is what is taught in "Chapter 1: Even If Your Toes Turn Purple." There is nothing your children can do in this world that will cause you to stop loving them. They need to know that they are safe, they are protected, and that you will have their backs no matter what happens. Saying these

> *We should teach our children to choose to be honorable*
> *men and women and to choose good, high paths.*

words to your children, and then living and proving it to them constantly, will help relieve the pressure you already have as parents. It will better equip you

Don't shame them—hug them.

to talk about the hard things with your children, and it will help them to be willing to put their trust in you.

Talk often, talk frequently, and talk openly.

ALEX'S ACTIONS

There are hard things for parents to talk about, and there are hard things for their kids to listen to. Sex is undoubtedly number one on the list, for parents and kids!

But that doesn't mean it shouldn't be talked about.

- Start talking openly with your kids at an early age. Then they'll be in a better position to have the conversations that really matter later on.

- Remember: Your kids are going to get the information they're looking for, and they're going to be better off if they get it from you.

Chapter 18

Avoiding the All or Nothing Trap

by Rich

Maintain proper balance and perspective.

Midway through my career in corporate America, I was given a leadership role in a large, international organization. I was eager and determined to earn my stripes, and I basically committed to do so at all costs. I was a very young general manager of the U.S. division, and I was driven to do anything that was necessary to succeed. My commitment bordered on insane. I had a young family, but I was traveling hundreds of thousands of miles every year. There were nights I would stay at the office all night long, sleeping on the floor to do what I felt needed to be done. I was going to succeed, and I didn't care about the costs.

Then I learned the lesson that it is not worth risking everything of importance in your life to achieve success. The division I was over was beginning to be highly successful. At this point, my mentor and boss, Dr. Peter Horne, had his secretary set up an urgent meeting with me. That meant jumping on a plane, flying to

Atlanta, then from Atlanta to Amsterdam, and from Amsterdam across the channel to Birmingham, England. Door-to-door, this was a twenty-and-a-half-hour trip. When I arrived, Dr. Horne's executive assistant ushered me into his office and sat me down.

Dr. Horne turned to me from his large desk and said, "Rich, we're really delighted with the progress you've made in the business. Things are coming along rather nicely." And then he made this comment, which hit me right on the nose: "This is not the reason I called you here today. Rich, I want you to remember one thing. You can replace almost anything in this world. You can replace a car. You can replace a job. You can replace money. But you can't replace your health, you can't replace your trust relationships, and, most importantly, you can't replace your family."

> *"You can't replace your health, you can't replace your trust relationships, and, most importantly, you can't replace your family."*

With piercing eyes, he dismissed me, waggling his hand at me and shooing me out of his office. That's it. I was called to Birmingham, England, for that five-minute conversation.

The next twenty-two-and-a-half hours gave me plenty of time to think about what Dr. Horne had just said. Most of my thoughts centered on my wife and children. For several years, I had been telling my wife, "This next project is a big one for me. I am going to give it my all for six months, so don't plan on seeing much of me. But once I finish it, things will be different." The six months would pass. I would complete the project, and then a new project would come along, and I would start the cycle all over again. Those six months had turned into years as I kept promising, "If I give my all to this for six months, then we will have it made." As we crossed the Atlantic, I reflected on a trip I had taken to India some months before. When I got home, all of my sons and I came down with whooping cough. We had all been immunized, but somehow we contracted this miserable illness. It was terrible. I remember coughing so hard one day that I literally vomited, but I lacked the discipline to take some time off from my work to get better and help my wife with our sons. My youngest son at the time was Nathan.  He was less than a year old when we all got sick, and it was life-threatening for him. In fact, he ended up in the hospital, where my wife took care of him because I was too busy.

Flying home, I realized I was falling into the "all or nothing trap," and I resolved that I was going to do better as a father and husband. When I got home, I made it a point to gather my young sons together, give them each a hug, and tell them I love them. But when I went to pick up Nathan, he hollered and screamed. As he pushed me away, I realized he did not even know who I was. At that moment, I realized that achieving my goal of being a CEO was not worth losing the love of my family. And I began to change both my priorities and how I actually lived my life.

Now, that doesn't mean I lost my intensity. It doesn't mean that I never end up out of balance. But my short session with Dr. Horne brought great clarity to the fact that it's not worth giving up the things that matter most for the things that matter least. Now, as I zig and zag from goal to goal, I will still put intense effort into achieving my dreams. But at each turn, I've established a reward that, for me, inevitably includes my family. (Your approaches, of course, may differ.) For each goal I pursue, I will set up guardrails that will determine the amount of time and effort I am willing to invest. There are not many ways to succeed without going out of balance for a period of time. The key is to realize that you are going out of balance for a short period and then bounce back and take some time off to enjoy your life.

My philosophy involves having a line of balance. Many people think you achieve this line of balance by being at work exactly at 8 a.m. and leaving within minutes of 5 p.m., by getting eight hours of sleep each night, and by controlling life with a rigid schedule. I don't live my life that way. At times I live my life extremely out of balance. I'll work so crazy hard that I think I'm going to die, and then I'll cross over and go for a cruise where I sleep eighteen hours a day. Then I'll charge back across the line and spend some incredible family time, then I'll go work my guts out again and literally not sleep for a couple of weeks while I start another new business. Then I'll spend a month in the Himalayas with my family. The way I define balance is not to try walking the perfect line but, rather, to cross that line of balance as frequently as possible. This is the final form of zigzagging I would suggest.

I am reminded of another unfortunate example of someone who charged straight toward a goal at all costs: an individual who completed his MBA program the same time I did. He was a charismatic and brilliant man. He had everything going for him— far more than the rest of us, really. During school and after we graduated, he was fixated on the same path I was on. He was going to the top, and he was going to succeed at all costs. I guess the only real difference between us is that I am fortunate enough to have a wife who has helped me become grounded and remember what really matters in my life.

This man was relentless in his pursuit of wealth. He racked up frequent flier miles and spent even more time away from his family than I did. He did whatever it took to get to the top, and he got there. In fact, by some measures, he has achieved a level of success I might have been envious of at one point in my life. But now, as I look back over my life and this man's life, I see some significant differences. He has been married and divorced multiple times. He has no relationship with his children; in fact, they will not even talk to him.

I look at him, and I am so grateful that Dr. Horne took the time to counsel with me—and then send me back on that transatlantic flight to think about what he said. As a result, my son Nathan—the one who would not let me touch him because he did not know who I was—now calls

> *As a result, my son . . . now calls me his hero.*

me his hero. Success is not worth heading over a cliff or getting so out of balance that we lose control. Everything in life requires balance. The best skiers cross that line of balance as often as possible as they race down the hill. But they know how to keep their momentum and stay upright through the race, rather than crashing and burning.

A key to maintaining our balance in life and in business is not getting so tightly wound up and so intense that we do not get in a rhythm, or what the best athletes call "flow." Many of us get so stressed and uptight that we create our own failures. Our stress then creates a form of reverse psychology, similar to what happens when I'm golfing and see a water hazard off to the left. Too often, I allow myself to think "Don't go left into the water," and just like that the ball invariably ends up going left, directly into the pond. If we get fixated on the things we think we can't do, or if we get consumed with the possibility of a little error or failure, we get wound up too tight. And that actually translates into negative behaviors that undercut our efforts.

Jeff Sandefer, a university professor and Harvard MBA who *Businessweek* named as one of the top entrepreneurship professors in the United States, spoke of a final exam he gave his MBA students. They were required to speak with ten seasoned and successful executives. Jeff further specified that the first three executives they interviewed needed to be highly successful but under the age of thirty-five. The next three successful executives were to be in their mid-forties and fifties. The final four interviews were to be with successful executives who were in the final stages of their careers. In each of the interviews, Jeff's students were to elicit information on how these executives pursued and viewed success.

Invariably, the young bucks were beating their chests and chasing after the brass ring, often in ways that put them at risk of losing their balance. The middle-aged executives were beginning to figure life out. Some of them had regrets, and others had chosen to add some balance to their lives.

Of course, it was the older executives who gave the real insight. It did not matter what type of business these men or women were involved with. In each case, they described a pattern of pursuing success that was guided by these three questions:

1) Was it honorable?
2) Did it leave an impact?
3) Who loves me, and who do I love?

Many of these older executives were billionaires. And yet they talked very little about money. What mattered to them was how their business helped others and whether their business mattered. They wanted to leave a legacy. And, most importantly, they talked about the people who loved them and the people they loved. Of course, there were those who did not have loved ones, and they talked about that absence with regret. They were honest and open and direct about their successes and their mistakes.

Whatever our goals are, whatever our beacon in the fog is, it is critical that we do what we do for the proper reasons and that we stay within the guardrails and values that we have set for ourselves. If we do, we will get to the end of our lives—which will inevitably come—and have no regrets.

1) Was it honorable?
2) Did it leave an impact?
3) Who loves me, and who do I love?

WHAT TO DO IF YOU'RE BEHIND IN THE GAME

I am frequently approached by a parent who expresses with sorrow that they are late to the game. They have a strained relationship with their

> *Let me boldly state that it is never too late!*

teen, or they were absent in the early years and don't know where to begin to make up for lost time. They wonder if it is too late.

Let me boldly state that it is never too late! We as humans are resilient, and most of the time, strained relationships can be mended. Here are the three things I would encourage:

1. Meet them at their level; don't expect them to go to your level.

Recently, Tim excitedly barged into our room close to midnight and shouted, "Dad, I need your help!"

I jumped up and said, "What are we doing son?"

"We need to win that Pokémon gym back."

I was tired, watching my favorite sitcom, and I did not want to go. Yet, I threw my shoes on, and we went and battled a Pokémon gym together. Did I do it because I wanted to be a Pokémon master? No! I did it because I wanted to meet Tim on his level and let him know that what matters to him matters to me. I have found that doing what he wants to do sometimes makes him value and want to listen to what I have to say.

Do what your children do! For me, this has included—but has not been limited to—marching band, football, soccer, bow and arrow shooting, Pokémon, debate, good music, terrible music, fishing, skiing, choir concerts, dance recitals, and the list goes on. The point is, take an interest in the things your teen is interested in. Avoid the tendency to choose or force the extracurricular activities that you enjoy or think would be best. Rather, let them show you their interests and talents. It is all right to encourage them to be involved, but never force them to participate in an activity that they do not want to be part of.

2. Be patient, but also be a parent.

If I have learned anything from my association with teens through the years, it is to be patient. They are often just trying to figure things out, and being patient and giving them latitude to learn and grow goes a long way.

Now this does not mean to be soft. Our children want us to be parents and set appropriate boundaries and limits; but pick the really important rules, and don't worry so much about the little, unimportant things. Your teen will not be perfect, and neither will you. Let them have the opportunity to be a teen and learn and grow from their small mistakes. Teach them to avoid the big mistakes.

3. Laugh.

The other day, one of Tim's good friends pulled a tub of chocolate chip cookie dough out of our freezer. He wanted to hide it from the other teens while allowing it to thaw, so he hid it in our oven—which was still cooling down.

Why would he do this? Well, he is a teenager . . . and that's how it rumbles when you're a teen. He went downstairs with the other teens and completely forgot about it. There it sat for two days until my wife turned the oven on to warm it up for some baking. You can only imagine the outcome.

Smoke billowed through the house, plastic melted on the bottom of the oven, cookie dough and the plastic lid mushroomed out of the bucket like the Stay Puft Marshmallow Man. What was my wife's first reaction? To be livid. Then what did she do? She laughed and laughed and laughed.

What do you think the result was with Tim's friend? Although he was embarrassed and felt like a dunce, he arrived at our home that night bearing a gift of dark chocolate, a fresh bin of homemade cookie dough, and the most tender apology note you have ever seen. He even cleaned up our entire kitchen.

So before you rage and rant, take a breath and ask yourself if laughing might be a more appropriate response.

I realize that some times relationships can be strained; but meeting them on their level, being patient, and laughing will go a long way to getting things back on track. Take ownership by seeking to understand first and then be understood. Most importantly, love them unconditionally.

ALEX'S ACTIONS

You can replace anything in this world but you can't replace your health, your trust relationships, and most importantly you can't replace your family.

Sometimes you have to work really hard or be out of balance, but if you long-term stay there, it damages these three most important things to protect in your life.

- Put guardrails in your life to avoid the all or nothing trap.

- Try to find a rhythm and flow. Over stressing or fixating on negative thoughts can cause you to self-destruct.

- At the end of your life being honorable, making an impact, and being loved and loving others is what will really matters.

Chapter 19

A Call for the
Teenagers of Today

by Tim

Kids can make a difference.

What do you want to do with your life? I don't know what I want to do with mine. We have so many options. We can become the first deep space explorers, or the first to cure cancer, or the first to invent a flying car—and the list goes on and on. We can do so much more than we can comprehend.

For the past two years, I've been talking to people about this book, and I've received a lot of mixed responses from adults. Many are excited for a teenager to be writing a book, and they are thrilled because they believe in us. Others have believed it to be a fun project that won't make it far. And then there are a few who have no faith in today's youth. They believe we are a trouble-making, dead generation. Honestly, I have no idea who is right, but I have faith that we will clean up our parents' mistakes and make the world a brighter place.

I've seen teens suffer from depression, anxiety, hate, envy, death, addictions, grief, and a lot of confusion. It's hard and sad to see someone drop to their knees and cry in the middle of the hall.

We have trials like no other generation. I've seen teens suffer from depression, anxiety, hate, envy, death, addictions, grief, and a lot of confusion. It's hard and sad to see someone drop to their knees and cry in the middle of the hall. It's hard to see someone who used to be so bright and happy turn into a slave to their bad habits. Sometimes we forget how much potential we actually have. Sometimes we forget the people who love us, and we make rash decisions that we wouldn't make with a little more thought. Even though we have our weaknesses, I know we are strong enough to overcome them.

To help deal with these challenges, I ask myself two questions every day: "Am I happy with who I am?" and "How can I show others who they are and what their potential is?" I've been asking myself these questions for seven years, and I've given myself a lot of different answers that have helped me become a better person.

The first question helps me realize that if I'm happy with who I am, then why does anything else matter? I know I am a good person, and no one can change that but myself. If I were not happy with myself, then I would try to change the things that I regret and work at them until I become the person I want to be. This isn't influenced by my peers or parents or anybody. I genuinely ask the question of *myself*. This makes me stay on the track I really want my life to be on.

Even though we have our weaknesses, I know we are strong enough to overcome them.

The second question, "How can I show others who they are and what their potential is?" is probably the hardest question anyone can ever ask. Instead of looking at people like you'd normally do, you have to change your whole perspective. You have to think of each person as a brother or sister. You have to learn to love a stranger. Acting on the answers you come up with is hard, but

If I'm happy with who I am, then why does anything else matter?

it's also the most rewarding thing anyone can ever experience. It brings true happiness to help a friend or a stranger out and to figure out who they are and their story.

Though it may be hard, we can always choose to be better than our parents. We can choose to be better than our circumstances. We can choose to be the best generation in all of history. I firmly believe that we all have a purpose and that we have unimaginable power to make a better world. I believe in you, and I have a bright hope for the future.

I don't know about you; but when I die, I want people to remember that I lived. I want my deeds and actions in this life to

You have to think of each person as a brother or sister. You have to learn to love a stranger.

impact someone in the next generation. I don't want to be a fleeting memory that is soon forgotten. While I live, I am going to make a difference! I don't know what I'm going to do when I grow up. I hardly know what I am going to do tomorrow; but maybe if I did something today that changes part of

a friend's world, and maybe if I did something small every day, I could change the whole world.

When I die, I want people to remember that I lived.

Chapter 20

The Truth about Teens

by Rich

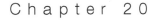

"The children . . . have bad manners, contempt for
authority; they show disrespect for elders and love
chatter in place of exercise."
—*Socrates*

As a small and squirrelly six-year-old, I had bright and inquiring
eyes. My father lost his sight to cancer when he was four years
old. He required me, his oldest child, to be uncharacteristical-
ly mindful. I saw for my father, verbalized our surroundings, and
then implemented his actions. This unusual childhood experience
required me to behave more like someone in his twenties than like
the youthful kid I was. It conditioned me to be deeply thoughtful
and endlessly inquisitive.

My curious nature led me to occasionally eavesdrop on three
of our neighbors. One cool spring afternoon, in particular, they
chatted across the neighborhood ditch. Never once did these three
agree with each other on any topic, from politics to the latest town
scandal. However, as the talk went on, there *was* one thing they

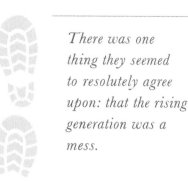

> *There was one thing they seemed to resolutely agree upon: that the rising generation was a mess.*

seemed to resolutely agree upon: that the rising generation was a mess. Kids were lazy and listened to Satan's music. The entire generation had lost its moral compass.

I recall the heaviness this caused me as a young, hopeful boy. My father calmed me with his observation and belief that each generation adapts from the one before, and each generation is just a little better than the one before. Our conversation gave me the confidence and peace to know that my father believed I was full of goodness and had a bright future.

I have observed through the years that adults generally think the rising generation is a mess. I have also observed that despite the old timers thinking youngsters have missed the mark, everyone seems to figure things out.

In April 2015, Roy H. Williams published a Monday Morning Memo titled "An Open Letter to 12-Year-Old Boys." It was profound! I required every employee and every young man that I worked with to read it. It reads:

An Open Letter to 12-Year-Old Boys

You're twelve.

Everyone treats you like a kid, but you and I know better, right?

You've known the difference between boys and girls for a lot longer than anyone suspects. But girls aren't the mystery you suppose them to be. They're far more mysterious than that. You're going to spend the rest of your life trying to figure out just one of them.

I remember twelve.

You're about to start getting a lot of advice from people who love you, and some of that advice will be pretty good. But you're also going to be told some things that are absolute crap.

You'll be told the secrets of success are to be smart and to work hard. But that's not entirely true. The world is full of successful people who rose to the top simply because they overcame their fear and took chances other people weren't willing to take.

Successful people usually fail multiple times before they succeed.

If working hard were the way to wealth, men who dig ditches in the heat of summer would be the wealthiest of us all.

We're paid according to the size of the responsibilities we've been entrusted to carry.

You'll be given responsibility when you demonstrate that you're willing to do what other people aren't willing to do. You're not going to want to do those things, either. But do them and do a good job. That's how you gain authority.

People will tell you that a single success can cause you to be "set for life" or that a single mistake can "ruin your life." But success and failure are both temporary conditions.

Grown-ups will tell you that you need to go to college to be successful. If you want to become an employee and climb the corporate ladder, college will definitely help you do that. But the downside of college is that it trains you to think like everyone else. If you want to leave your fingerprints on the world you're going to need to have your own way of thinking.

Good decisions come from experience, and experience comes from bad decisions. So never be afraid to experiment. Just make sure you can afford to fail.

People will tell you that you need to "find your purpose." But this would lead you to believe that you have only ONE purpose and that it's a secret.

Piffle and pooh. You don't need to find a purpose; you need to choose one.

You fall in love with a purpose exactly like you fall in love with a girl: by reaching out and touching it each day. When you make daily contact with something, it becomes an important part of your life. You make your mark on it, and it makes its mark on you.

You'll be told that you must plan your work and work your plan. But the winners are those who know how to improvise when things don't go according to plan.

You can choose what you want to do, but you can't choose the consequences.

There's a big difference between the way things ought to be and the way things really are. If you moan about how things ought to be, you're a whiner. And the only people who like whiners are other whiners.

But if you work to make things better, you're an activist. If you fling yourself headlong into making things better, you're a revolutionary. Congratulations, you found a purpose.

Grown-ups with good intentions will tell you that you should "enjoy these years of no responsibility, blah, blah, blah." But grown-ups who have warm and fuzzy memories of the years between twelve and sixteen aren't remembering those years as well as they think.

It's pretty cool when you can hop into a car and go anywhere you want to go. But after a few years you'll realize that no place is quite as special as the place you came from. But you can never really go home again because "home" changes just like you do. This is what Heraclitus meant when he said you can't step into the same river twice.

The best advice I can give you is that you should marry your best friend and never let anyone or anything be more important to you than her. If you've always got your best friend with you, life is pretty amazing.

Hang in there, kid.
And remember what I told you.
Roy H. Williams

I've been blessed with five amazing sons. And I haven't spent their teenage years living in fear of them taking bad paths. Have there been bumps, bruises, and mistakes? Of course! But my experience is that their souls are strong and vibrant, and they want to do good. On any given night, there can be anywhere from five to twenty young men in my home for dinner. Sometimes they even invite a few young ladies. We particularly enjoy these nights. I find the teens I know to be respectful, thoughtful, kind, tender, helpful, highly intelligent, and, for the record, a thousand times better than I or any of my friends were at their age. I think the burden is more on us as parents and adults to give these youth the mechanisms, the grounding, and the guidance they need to be the best that they can be. I do not think that the teenagers are something to be feared but, rather, to be celebrated.

I *have* noticed that teenagers' BS detectors are highly attuned. You can't bamboozle teenagers—they know when someone or something is trying to manipulate them. If they understand an adult's intent and purpose, they engage eagerly enough. But try giving them a task without a cause or a vision, and you have already stuck a fork in the project. If you're sincere, real, genuinely interested, and loving, they will not only trust in and communicate with you, but they will also build and uplift you.

> But my experience is that their souls are strong and vibrant, and they want to do good.

Maybe teenagers are a lot like us. Maybe they're even a lot like my cranky neighbors who griped across the neighborhood ditch! We adults are actually nothing more than teenagers trying to act mature.

Each generation has its challenges, difficulties, and hurdles. Whether we're 82, 51, 26, or 13, we all have the same deep needs: to live, to love, to learn, and to matter.

I've heard many parents express panic, fear, and concern for their teenagers and declare how confident they are that their teens will make such serious mistakes that they are certain they are going to lose some of their children. Do I think that the potential pitfalls and problems are more extreme than ever? Yes. But I also think teenagers are stronger souls than they've ever been!

The modern world runs at such an accelerated pace. Our teens *can't* behave the same as prior generations or they will not survive.

Take, for example, the pace of revolutions. On July 4, 1776, approximately 150 copies of the Declaration of Independence were distributed, but no one signed it on this date. As a matter of fact, it wasn't signed in its entirety until August 2, 1776. It took almost a month to distribute the document, get the word out, and get it signed. Contrast that with July 2, 2013, when 16 people were killed and 200 injured in protests at Cairo University against the then-Egyptian president, Mohammed Morsi. Morsi was deposed the next day—July 3, 2013—due to the immediate social media blitz surrounding the events.

> *Our teens can't behave the same as prior generations or they will not survive.*

A completed revolution in a day! That's 1/56 the time it took for the USA to *announce* its revolution, let alone fight for it. How can we expect our children and teens *not* to behave differently, to adapt, to find new methods and new models?

How many messages hit us (especially our teens) each day? How do we process them? How do we manage the stimulus overload? Is this rapid-fire messaging and information overload good or bad? I contend it is both. For example, are cell phone interruptions all bad? There's certainly a lack of attention due to cell phones, but look at the response time we now have at our fingertips!

It's so important to give teens and ourselves quiet moments; however, it is also vital we understand that, just as our grandparents adapted to automobiles, we adjusted to the communication age, and our children have and will continue to adjust to developing technology.

We do face a values epidemic, but it isn't the first time. We need to give our children hope in the future amidst the many fears the world has to offer. As we

> *We do face a values epidemic, but it isn't the first time.*

bond together as families, as we enact the values discussed in this book, I am confident that our teens will be better and stronger than us, that they will make changes in the world that we can't even dream of.

I remember when my wife was pregnant with my oldest son in 1990. We were so excited to be having our first child, yet I also remember the uncontrollable fear my wife and I faced as the Iraqi Gulf War was unfolding. My wife's brother who was closest to her in age was in the Armed Forces and preparing to launch an attack against the royal guard of Saddam Hussein. Indeed, his division was to be one of the first across the border, leading the attack. We were told to expect one in four of the soldiers in that conflict to die. This was particularly sensitive to us because her brother had a wife and a baby the same age as ours. My wife and I shared our feelings with each other and questioned how we could dare bring a child into this crazy, upside-down world.

As I conferred with my wise, loving, tender mother, she relieved with me her experience when she was pregnant with me. I was born on July 5, 1964.

In the month I was born, the USSR performed a nuclear test at Eastern Kazakh/Semipalatinsk USSR. Barry Goldwater, an openly bigoted individual, declared his presidential candidacy. The USA fired shots at North Vietnam, putting that conflict into full gear. A Rolling Stones concert was halted in Ireland after twelve minutes due to riots. Meanwhile, race riots were flaring up across the United States. In that month, specifically, there was a riot in

Rochester, New York, that killed four people. To top it off, union leader James Hoffa was sentenced for fraud, and 800 University of California students were arrested for protesting.

My mother proclaimed, "This is the world that I brought you into, son."

As warped as it sounds, our conversation gave me comfort and soothed me considerably as she walked me through the warped events of her time. Free sex, drugs, and rock 'n' roll! Woodstock in all its glory. Vietnam. Cuban protests. Missiles pointed at the United States. The Bay of Pigs. Ugh.

With deep sincerity in her eyes, my mother said, "My precious, oldest son and my sweetheart new daughter, it will work out fine."

Fast-forward twenty-five years, and my oldest son John just graduated from university. Have there been some bumps and bruises? Sure; but his life has been amazing and full of great experiences and wonderful adventures. I could not imagine not having brought this child (or any of my other sons) into this world! Everything has a way of working out. I have concluded that, in reality, the world we live in has always been upside-down—particularly when we bother to look at things with a scrutinizing eye.

Recently I turned fifty-one. I was delighted as my family gathered around to express their love and tenderness to me. I have been very blessed that my second son, Matthew, is married to his true love, a delightful, amazing young woman named Heather. I adore this new

> *I could not imagine not having brought this child (or any of my other sons) into this world!*

daughter-in-law as much as (if not more than) I would if she were my own flesh-and-blood daughter. As we began the ceremony of going around the room, with each member of the family presenting me with their gift, I received a card, as well as a wrapped square plaque, from Matthew and Heather. They expressed their love and appreciation to me. After this point, they then strongly insisted that

I open the card and read very carefully first. The card read, "What do you give a man who has absolutely every toy he wants? I guess you have to give him something he has never had before."

As I opened the second gift, the unwrapped plaque read, "Married February 13, 1987; father December 26, 1990; grandfather March 2016! To the world's new greatest grandfather!"

My wife jumped up and danced around the floor in light of the announcement. Tears welled up in our eyes, and we celebrated the joyful news with a group family hug. After dinner and all the festivities, we were able to sit with Matthew and Heather, and they were able to share their feelings about the pregnancy with us. Heather expressed how excited and joyful she was to bring this child into the world; however, both expressed their fear and trepidation.

"The world is upside-down and so crazy right now. There are evil (and legal) judicial rulings, and there are financial insecurities through all the world. ISIS is trying to kill Westerners. There's global warming, Ebola, and the disintegration of the family and the core values the family represents. We're just a little bit nervous with the state of the world and bringing this precious child into it."

At that moment, the wisdom and tenderness that my mother had passed on to me, with both her actions and her words, returned to me, and I shared them with Heather and Matthew. Gratefully, it had the same calming effect on them that it did me those twenty-six years prior.

Regretfully, the story does not end happily. The following week, Heather had severe pains and lost the baby. In a matter of one week, they went from being ecstatic about having a precious child to having a miscarriage, and thus experiencing a loss of that source of joy. To compound these events, Heather's life was put in jeopardy, and my son and daughter-in-law were saddled with hospital bills double

They weathered the trial with a firm belief of the good that will come their way. They looked to the future and won.

the cost of what it would have been to have a child and bring it home.

As sad and sorrowful as this situation was for Matthew and Heather, I am extremely proud of their resilience and their accepting the arduous hardship with hope and a deeper understanding of our mortal condition. They weathered the trial with a firm belief of the good that will come their way. They looked to the future and won.

I have found, as I've grown to be an older man, that I'm a little bit more emotional and tender. I now seem to view things in the long term, no longer so heavily focused on the present! As I reflected on things that night, I thought of a song that was sung at our wedding: "A Long Line of Love" by Michael Martin Murphey. The beautiful lyrics of this song are consistent with Roy's message, as well as the advice my mother gave my wife and me years ago. The most significant things we can offer our children are belief, stability, and a loving, safe family environment.

Let's remember where we started this book: "Even if your toes turn purple." Let's show our teens unconditional love! Let's make sure they know we are in their court. Yes, hold them accountable and have appropriate discipline; but never let them doubt that we love them and believe in them. Let's take an intense interest in them and give them hope for the future, even with the many fears the world has to offer.

The truth is, teens are terrific. And this next generation has the chance to solve many world problems that we cannot even get our adult brains around. Love your teens, celebrate with them, and enjoy every second of these precious years.

Index

Made in the USA
Lexington, KY
03 July 2017